AMERICAN ATROCITY

AMERICAN ATROCITY

THE TYPES OF VIOLENCE IN LYNCHING

GUY LANCASTER

The University of Arkansas Press
Fayetteville
2021

ISBN: 978-1-68226-186-6
eISBN: 978-1-61075-755-3

25 24 23 22 21   5 4 3 2 1

Manufactured in the United States of America

Designed by Liz Lester

♾ The paper used in this publication meets the minimum requirements
of the American National Standard for Permanence of Paper
for Printed Library Materials Z39.48-1984.

Library of Congress Cataloging-in-Publication Data

Names: Lancaster, Guy, 1976– author.
Title: American atrocity: the types of violence in lynching /
Guy Lancaster.
Description: Fayetteville: The University of Arkansas Press, 2021. |
Includes index. | Summary: "Drawing from the fields of history,
philosophy, cognitive science, sociology, and literary theory, and quoting
chilling contemporary accounts, historian Guy Lancaster argues that the
act of lynching encompasses five distinct but overlapping types
of violence"—Provided by publisher.
Identifiers: LCCN 2021010730 | ISBN 9781682261866 (paperback) |
ISBN 9781610757553 (ebook)
Subjects: LCSH: Lynching—United States—History. | Violence—United
States—History. | African Americans—United States—History.
Classification: LCC HV6457 .L35 2021 | DDC 364.1/34—dc23
LC record available at https://lccn.loc.gov/202101073

CONTENTS

INTRODUCTION

Why did her tears reveal to me what I had learned long ago, but had forgotten in my frenzied love, that there is a draught that we must drink or not be fully human? I knew that one must know the truth. I knew quite well that when one is adult one must raise to one's lips the wine of the truth, heedless that it is not sweet like milk but draws the mouth with its strength, and celebrate communion with reality . . .

—Rebecca West, *The Return of the Soldier*

AT PRESENT IN THE UNITED STATES, awareness of our shared history of racialized violence is growing, along with a desire to commemorate—that is, to remember together—that violence by installing markers in public places or developing classroom curricula to teach younger generations what earlier ones often learned only through the whispers of their own elders. The Equal Justice Initiative, for one, has been prominent in the public conversation, releasing its *Lynching in America* study in 2015 and then, three years later, opening the National Memorial for Peace and Justice in Montgomery, Alabama, a site dedicated to the memory of those who suffered slavery, lynching, segregation, and more. But there has also been an array of state- and community-focused efforts. In Arkansas, for example, the centennial of the Elaine Massacre of 1919, part of the infamous "Red Summer," was commemorated with a monument to the dead in Phillips County and a number of public events, including conferences and workshops, all across the state. Meanwhile, in advance of the centennial of the Tulsa Race Riot of 1921, experts in Oklahoma began carrying out forensic research with the aim of uncovering any mass graves that may exist. Representation of these events is even entering popular culture, with the massacre at Tulsa a cornerstone for the HBO television series *Watchmen* (2019) and *Lovecraft Country* (2020). These trends reached a crescendo in the spring of 2020 with the demonstrations following the killing of George Floyd by police officers in Minneapolis, Minnesota. Across the world, discussions of structural or systematic racism came to the fore in a way they never had previously, as exemplified best by the author Kimberly Jones, who, in one video viewed millions of times following the "rioting" in Minneapolis, specifically cited anti-Black violence at Tulsa in 1921 and at Rosewood, Florida, in 1923 as historical violations of the social contract that have fed into the present moment.[1]

The public hunger for information on lynching and other cases of racialized violence has fueled, and been fueled by, an expanding output of scholarship in the disciplines of history, sociology, political science, literary studies, and others. In my own research, however, I have had to confront what might be called the limits of typology, or the fact that the terms we use to characterize various cases of racialized violence—lynching, race riot, massacre, pogrom, racial cleansing, nightriding/whitecapping—constitute less discrete categories and more a blurred spectrum.[2]

Even more, the word *lynching* itself cannot be considered a discrete practice but, instead, covers multiple forms of violence. And by that, I do not mean only that lynching may be carried out using either a noose or a gun, practiced against either the mythical "Black beast" or against white horse thieves, and perpetrated either by a quiet band in the dead of night or by a whole town on the public square in the light of day. Instead, I mean that lynching, as a practice, accords with several different "big picture" frameworks for understanding violence, frameworks that theorists have produced across a spectrum of disciplines. These models of violence are not mutually exclusive—in fact, they reinforce each other quite well and offer a variety of perspectives that provide a much deeper understanding of what lynching was and what its perpetrators wanted to accomplish.

That, then, is the motivation behind this book— to illustrate concisely the types of violence within the category of lynching, and to demonstrate how we might apply these models, especially for those who may not be aware of the wealth of theory regarding the origin and nature of violence.

Chapter 1 will explicate lynching as group violence. Here, I must beg the reader's indulgence somewhat, for it will be necessary to survey an array of scholarly literature on the nature of groups themselves in order to explain why *group violence*, as opposed to a very similar concept like *collective violence*, is the better framework for understanding the nature of lynching. While lynching has popularly been portrayed as the act of vigilantes or committed racists, perpetrated against either isolated individuals or small groups accused of wrongdoing, this chapter will reveal lynching to be, especially in its racialized manifestations, the violence of one group against another. Lynch mobs were not operating at the lawless fringes of culture but were, instead, immersed in the broader, deeper culture of white supremacy. Moreover, when the mob lynched a man or woman, they did not just punish that one person—they terrorized entire communities.

Chapter 2 analyzes lynching as objective or structural violence. This study builds upon the works of Johan Galtung and Slavoj Žižek to illustrate how lynching was not the eruption of violence into a peaceful world but, instead, the manifestation of a broader system of inequality and oppression. Such a representation of lynching will hinge largely upon a study of Act 258 of 1909, an Arkansas law that attempted to substitute mob violence with the expedited judgment of the court as a means of preventing lynching, while doing exactly nothing to punish the mobs for murder or to sanction officers of the law who failed to protect their charges from the wrath of vigilantes.

While lynching, like other forms of collective violence such as genocide, is frequently described as being possible only because of the persistent "dehumanization" of the victims-to-be, in chapter 3 I will argue that lynching actually constitutes humanistic violence. In fact, recognizing the humanity of the lynching victim was necessary for the mobs to receive the greatest satisfaction from their deeds. Borrowing from the works of Fritz Breithaupt, Kate Manne, and others, I intend to demonstrate that lynching parties were quite aware of the humanity of their intended victims—and sought to destroy them precisely because of it.

Chapter 4 builds upon the virtuous violence theory of Alan Page Fiske and Tage Shakti Rai, who have argued, rather convincingly, that perpetrators often perform violent deeds out of a sense that they are morally right.

Violence, the theorists demonstrate, can be employed to honor, create, and sustain social relationships, and this certainly pertains to lynching, which was often justified by reference to a defense of the (white) community. Members of the mob often regarded their own deeds as heroic, and if the newspapers of the time and place did not always attach such labels to their deeds, they at least—and quite often—portrayed the victim of lynching as representing the purest form of evil possible, thus rendering the mob a virtuous collective by contrast.

The final chapter offers a synthesis of the previous four by analyzing lynching through the lens of René Girard's mimetic theory of violence. According to Girard, it is the nature of human beings to imitate the desires of others, which can lead to rivalry when desires converge upon the same object. This rivalry can encompass others, threatening the entire community, with peace being restored only through the mechanism of a scapegoat whose guilt is universally agreed upon. In the United States, African Americans have regularly functioned as this scapegoat, especially as they were regarded by many white men as exhibiting mimetic desire for white women. Mimetic violence is thus both humanistic, in that it attributes human qualities to its victims, as well as collective, in that it is perpetrated by a group for the restoration of its peace—which makes said violence a virtue, too. In addition, the violent regulation of perceived desires following the Civil War was a function not only of vigilantes but also of the state, which instituted various anti-miscegenation measures to prevent cross-racial romance and solidarity, thus making violence aimed at regulating such relationships an example of objective or structural violence.

To some, this book could well seem extraneous to the broader concerns of scholars who make a study of racial violence. After all, what does it mean to study lynching? For the many sociologists and historians who have led the way in this field, studying lynching has entailed trying to understand the individual and collective motivation of perpetrators, the specific cultural contexts that made lynching viable and allowed perpetrators to escape punishment, the identity of the victims and therefore the reasons they may have been chosen for extermination, the geographical and temporal variability of the practice, how lynching affected the targeted communities, and which methods used to combat lynching ultimately proved successful and why. In addition, throughout the decades, literary historians like Trudier Harris and Koritha Mitchell, political scientists such as Daniel Kato, rhetoricians such as Ersula J. Ore and Megan Eatman, and theologians like James H. Cone and Angela D. Sims have expanded the questions we can ask relating to such performances of racial violence. However, despite all the tremendous work that has been and continues to be done on the subject of lynching, we nonetheless lack the same attempt at a unifying body of theory that one can find in other interdisciplinary fields such as genocide studies. Works such as Christopher Waldrep's 2002 book *The Many Faces of Judge Lynch: Extralegal Violence and Punishment in America* are tremendously valuable in tracking the evolution of the concept of lynching and demonstrating that the word has historically been applied not to one discrete phenomenon but to an array of them. Recognizing the historical mutability of definitions, however, does not necessarily help us at our present moment if we want to commemorate a lynching in the public space and create some shared understanding of America's record of racial violence. Doing that requires asking exactly what kind of violence was present in lynching—the intention of the present book.

For my part, theory is not an indulgent scholarly exercise untethered from the concerns of historical and sociological evidence but, instead, simply an attempt to be precise with the words that we use. Consider the term *lynching*. If you were to consult your thesaurus, you might encounter a variety of related words such as *murder*, *homicide, assassination, killing, slaying, slaughter, massacre, carnage*, and more. But all of these words have a somewhat different flavor, have different connotations, and thus produce differing value judgments when encountered. *Homicide*, for example, carries with it the connotation of police investigations or official statistics, but lynching rarely entailed such investigations outside the typical coroner's report that the death in question occurred "at the hands of persons unknown." Moreover, it was not police departments or state agencies that compiled statistics of lynching but, instead, activist groups and journalists fighting a reign of racial terror.

Likewise, consider the term *murder*. The word can be used synonymously with *homicide* but also comes with an array of statutory definitions that specifically characterize the type of homicide in question, be it first-degree murder versus second-degree or murder with malice aforethought. Lynch mobs were homicidal, and lynchings were murders, but this does not make these terms equivalent. As the historian James R. McGovern put it: "While murder is usually a personal deed, lynching, in the sense of the execution of another person by a self-constituted group with accompanying public rituals, is a social act; it requires confidence in community approval."[3]

Similarly, let us consider the term *assassination*. An assassination is a murder, but the terms have specific connotations that mean they are not exactly interchangeable. The assassin, in our mind, typically murders from a place of concealment and/or murders a particularly prominent individual, usually for political motivations. We may typically envision a lone gunman like Lee Harvey Oswald, although the killers of Julius Caesar constituted something of a mob who carried out their deed, like many lynchings, in the full light of day. But *assassination* is not synonymous with *lynching* for a variety of reasons, especially given that assassins rarely if ever engaged in the grisly rituals associated with many lynchings.

Execution denotes something that comes after a trial and sentencing and was originally defined as carrying out a legal order. While the word occasionally would be used in lynching reports, perhaps in part to lend vigilantism the veneer of process, a lynching was most certainly not an execution in the sense of having legal validity; and, as we will see in chapter 2, the state worked hard to substitute legal killings for the illegal. Meanwhile, words like *slaughter* and *massacre* suggest multiple victims of killing and thus, typically, violence against a collective rather than an individual. Lynching could certainly entail such violence but more often manifested itself in the murder of one person—even if, as we will see in chapter 1, the goal was to affect the broader community as a whole.

In other words, these various terms describe types of violence that can be differentiated in important ways, even if they do overlap in others. Thus, it is the aim of the present volume to elucidate the manner in which lynching was unique by exploring the various forms of violence manifest in it. Such an understanding should facilitate discussions about how we remember lynching, how we present it in the historical record, and how we commemorate it in public spaces.

As many scholars have already argued, no one definition of lynching can encompass the diversity of acts and motivations to which that term has applied. It is thus not my intent to fashion some definition that can encompass all the historical uses of the term. Words change meaning in subtle ways over time. Watch a play by William Shakespeare, and you will encounter words used in ways at variance from their present meaning. *Rogue*, for example, originally denoted a tramp or vagabond, but now the term is regularly applied to people who bravely "buck the system." Likewise, the term *lynching* once denoted a range of vigilante violence, not always lethal, perpetrated for purposes of "community regulation." However, the term has evolved significantly, and it will therefore be helpful to provide a working definition for the purposes of guiding our survey. As anthropologist Veena Das writes, "Naming the violence does not reflect semantic struggles alone—it reflects the point at which the body of language becomes indistinguishable from that of the world; the act of naming constitutes a performative utterance."[4] Given the types of violence covered in this book, I propose the following definition:

Lynching is

+ a scapegoating form of lethal violence;
+ performed by one group of human beings against another group of human beings (or an individual representing said group) assigned lower moral status;
+ for purposes regarded as virtuous by its

perpetrators, such as punishment and regulation;

* with the effect of maintaining the very structural inequalities that delineate group boundaries and their respective moral statuses.

Throughout this book, I will be pulling a variety of examples from the history of Arkansas. This is not because I consider Arkansas the most representative state from which to draw material, although an argument could, perhaps, be made for such a position, especially since Arkansas contains lowland areas that culturally and economically gravitate toward the Deep South and upland areas more representative of Appalachia, with even some bleed-over into the Midwest. Instead, I want to demonstrate the applicability of these frameworks within a relatively limited geographical area—and thus avoid the appearance of simply picking and choosing the best examples from the whole of American history. Besides, this is also the state with which I am most familiar, and thus I can provide a range of applicable examples, from well-documented spectacle lynchings that have attracted considerable researcher attention, to more obscure events only traceable through isolated sources.[5]

In addition, this book will focus primarily upon the lynching of African Americans by whites. While there were white-on-white lynchings, as well as cases of Black vigilantism upon fellow African Americans, and, at least in Arkansas, one rare instance of Black-on-white mob violence, the fact is that lynching mostly has been a mechanism for the social control of African Americans. In fact, recent work in Arkansas, such as that by historian Kelly Houston Jones on the lynching of slaves, has begun to revise many of our assumptions about the nature of vigilantism and has revealed, contrary to expectations, that lynching was heavily racialized even in the antebellum years.

As I will discuss in this book's conclusion, the decades separating that time period when lynching was shockingly common from the present moment, combined with the strategies employed by activists to shame a nation into confronting racialized violence, have left us a distorted view of what exactly constituted lynching, as both an act and an idea. Lynching entailed a much greater structure of violence than is typically acknowledged. Revealing that— and thus celebrating communion with reality, no matter how horrifying—is the intention of this book.

1

GROUP

*"Don't you make any mistake about it; if you will
have it that I killed the boy, then you've killed him
as much as I."*

*In sincerity of feeling and openness of statement,
these words went far beyond anything that had
ever been said in this home, kept up on the wages
of a secret industry eked out by the sale of more
or less secret wares: the poor expedients devised by
a mediocre mankind for preserving an imperfect
society from the dangers of moral and physical
corruption, both secret, too, of their kind.*

—Joseph Conrad, *The Secret Agent*

GIVEN THAT THIRTEEN PEOPLE were murdered over
the course of four days in and around a town that had
probably at most two hundred residents, we know shockingly
little about what happed at St. Charles in southeastern
Arkansas in the spring of 1904. As the historian Vincent
Vinikas writes, "Circumstances surrounding the event are
untraceable in the public record, and, apart from the facts
conveyed in a very limited number of sources, the available
material provides only a few other clues for historians. The
evidence is so flawed and scanty that it is hard to reconstruct

a sequence of events: questions of who, what, when, and how are virtually unanswerable, and any suggestion of why is wild conjecture."[1] However, what occurred may have been, depending upon the definition of *lynching* employed, one of the deadliest lynchings in the United States.

As Vinikas has reconstructed from a variety of sources, the mass lynching in St. Charles in late March 1904 apparently had its genesis in a round of drinking and gaming that turned into an argument down on the docks of the White River. A Black man, surnamed Griffin, delivered a blow to the head of a white man named Jim Searcy. The officer who arrested Griffin apparently indicated that Griffin might possibly be lynched, which frightened the captive so much that he struck the officer, stole his gun, and ran for his life. Newspapers, of course, told a slightly different story. According to the *Arkansas Gazette*, for example, "the difficulty occurred over a trivial matter ... between a white man by the name of Searcy and two negroes by the names of Henry and Walker Griffin." One of the Griffins threatened "to knock Searcy in the head with a beer bottle" but apparently did not. Then, on Monday, March 21, the two Griffins met Searcy and his brother in a store, whereupon one of the Griffins "struck both of the Searcy boys over the head with a table leg, rendering them unconscious and fracturing their skulls." A deputy sheriff was also knocked down.

The *Gazette* report contains an odd few lines describing the deeds of various actors after this affair: "The negroes then gathered and defied the officers, declaring 'no white man could arrest them.' Their demonstrations aroused the fears of the citizens of St. Charles, and they phoned to this place [the county seat of DeWitt] for a posse to come out and protect the town." According to the

Gazette's own reporting, the fight between the Griffins and the Searcys took place on Monday, but a deputy sheriff did not set out from DeWitt to St. Charles "to protect the town" until Wednesday morning, which fact perhaps suggests that locals did not consider whatever happened that Monday to be of too great an importance until time and rumor allowed a growing panic to build—a lull of this sort often precedes the actual violence. Whatever the case, when this deputy sheriff led a posse of five men to St. Charles on March 23, they encountered three armed African American men. The posse asked these men the location of Griffin but then shot them dead when the three reportedly "attempted to draw their pistols."

Large mobs of white men began to pour in from DeWitt, Clarendon, and other towns surrounding St. Charles. On March 24, a sheriff killed one Black man who supposedly shot at his posse. In addition, white authorities in St. Charles arrested five African Americans on unspecified charges, the *Gazette* reporting only that they "had defied the officers." That night, "a crowd of men took them away from the guards and shot them to death." By the end of the week, the *Gazette* headline blared, "Eleven Negroes Victims of Mob," although its summary of events does little to illuminate the nature of the violence. For example, this is the full report on one of the casualties covered: "Kellis Johnson, the last of the gang of negroes that caused the trouble, was shot to death this morning in the northeastern part of the county."[2] What is one to make of that? In his analysis of this event, Vinikas admits: "The lynchers in Saint Charles left a trail that cannot be mapped in even its basic directions. Because of the magnitude of inconsistency, error, and omission in the evidentiary base upon which researchers must rely, when or where or why particular killings occurred can only be deduced, inferred, or guessed. The path of the terror is lost in time and place."[3] The Griffins were apparently killed later, bringing the total dead to thirteen.

Most reports on what happened at St. Charles describe it as a lynching, but as Vinikas writes, "The word *lynch* is seriously flawed. When the term is employed to denote a specific category of human experience, it is not only imprecise, as one soon discovers; it is also . . . too clean."[4] Especially as employed in the American context, the term *lynching* can evoke either the "rough justice" of the American West dished out to outlaws or an explicitly racialized form of violence that, despite being couched in terms of justice or righteous vengeance, was often employed symbolically against entire communities. The term grew out of a practice, and that practice evolved depending upon time and place, thus creating a challenge for the continued application of our terminology. In addition, as Vinikas notes, "Regardless of its definition, when violence turns into a killing spree—as occurred in Saint Charles over the course of several days in the spring of 1904—isolating and defining the discrete historical event is difficult but statistically significant. Does the rampage count as one incident or several?"[5] But his question has more than simple statistical applicability, for it raises other questions as to the nature of the violence practiced. Do we regard what happened at St. Charles as violence against a collection of individuals, or do we define it as violence against a group or community? And if the latter, how many individuals must be targeted for violence before we treat this as a case of group violence—or can one such killing be considered a case of group violence, especially in the times and places where lynching was the order of the day?

These issues have long troubled those studying the practice. As historian Christopher Waldrep has written, "There is no single behavior that can be called 'lynching.' Any attempt to impose a definition on such a diverse, subtle, and complex reality will inevitably miss the point."[6] American studies professor Ashraf H. A. Rushdy identifies three main problems with the term *lynching*. First, it is "a term more evocative than descriptive," connoting, depending upon time and place, "quite different historical acts among the population." Second, "this same term has been used to designate acts that demonstrate a wide range of diverse motives, strategies, technologies, and meanings," including both lethal and nonlethal violence, as well both "acts of rough justice in frontier societies lacking the apparatus of state judiciaries as well as acts of direct defiance of those state judiciaries in more established societies." Finally, *lynching* "is a politically encumbered term" that has, through its history, both implied "popular sovereignty and Southern honor" and the failure of civilization.[7]

However, since the practice began attracting scholarly analysis in the early twentieth century, most definitions created to describe the phenomenon have emphasized the communal nature of the perpetrators. Economist James Cutler, who published the first scholarly analysis of lynching in 1905, emphasized the popular support enjoyed by vigilantism when he defined lynching as "an illegal and summary execution at the hands of a mob, or a number of persons, who have in some degree the public opinion of the community behind them."[8] In 1940, delegates at a conference attended by the National Association for the Advancement of Colored People (NAACP), the Association of Southern Women for the Prevention of Lynching (ASWPL), and the International Labor Defense (ILD) developed a definition of lynching composed of four specific components: "(1) there must be evidence that a person was killed, (2) the person must have met his death illegally, (3) three or more persons must have participated in the killing, [and] (4) the group must have acted under the pretext of service to justice or tradition."[9] In other words, as historian W. Fitzhugh Brundage notes, "a degree of community approval and complicity, whether expressed in popular acclaim for the mob's actions or in the failure of law enforcement either to prevent lynching or to prosecute lynchers, was present in most lynchings."[10] Rushdy himself, despite the problems he acknowledges inhering to any definition of lynching, offers the following capacious definition: "A lynching is an act of extralegal collective violence by a group alleging pursuit of summary justice."[11]

What these various definitions have in common is their emphasis upon lynching as violence carried out either by a group or, at the very least, on behalf of a group. In this respect, we can describe lynching as a form of *collective* violence, but this falls somewhat short of the reality of lynching, which should be better understood as a form of *group* violence. As sociologists James Hawdon and John Ryan define it, "group violence is broader than what is typically covered in works on collective violence because it includes violence *committed by collectives or groups* as well as violence *committed against groups*."[12] And group violence is not merely violence against multiple people but implies something about the relationship assumed between those targeted. "Crimes against humanity do not target humanity, but groups of human beings," writes philosopher Paul Dumouchel.[13]

This dynamic comes to the fore especially with a case such as that of St. Charles in 1904, for the kind of violence exhibited there easily bleeds over into what is typically called a "race riot." Although there are debates about what, if anything, differentiates a race riot from a lynching, economist Gunnar Myrdal, for one, regarded such riots as "magnified, or mass, lynchings," saying that the ultimate effect of the riot was the same as the lynching.[14] The historian Gilles Vandal, however, makes the following distinction: "Lynching is habitually the killing of one or more persons who is/are seized and illegally executed for an alleged crime, while a riot usually involves the haphazard killing of people at random by a mob under strong excitement."[15] For political scientist Donald L. Horowitz, the race riot (or, to use his term, the deadly ethnic riot) can be defined as "an intense, sudden, though not wholly unplanned, lethal attack by civilian members of one ethnic group on civilian members of another ethnic group, the victims chosen because of their group membership."[16]

Such a riot consists of four components:

1. "rumors of aggression inflicted *by* the target group," often employed "in setting a crowd on a course of mass violence *against* the target group";
2. a momentary lull that "occurs mainly in cases where the last precipitant comes on suddenly and the question is what to make of it";
3. a period of preparation during which would-be rioters begin to arm themselves; and
4. the atrocity killing, the riot itself.[17]

According to political scientist Ann V. Collins, race riots are "rational, extralegal, relatively short eruptions of white-on-black violence aimed at influencing social change."[18] Such riots only occur when three specific preconditions are met: "certain *structural factors*—primarily demographic, economic, labor, political, legal, social, and institutional features; *cultural framing*, or actions and discourse by both whites and blacks to further their own causes; and a *precipitating event*, the immediate spark that ignites the violence."[19]

Vinikas himself regularly uses the term *massacre* to describe the events at St. Charles, and although the term has not been as thoroughly explored as has *lynching*, there is a growing body of scholarship working to analyze massacres independent of a genocidal or wartime context. Historians Philip G. Dwyer and Lyndall Ryan, for example, define a massacre as

> the killing by one group of people by another group of people, regardless of whether the victims are helpless or not, regardless of age or sex, race, religion and language, and regardless of political, cultural, racial, religious or economic motives for the killing. The killing can be either driven by official state policy or can occur as a result of the state's lack of control over those groups or collectives on the ground. Massacres, in other words, can occur with or without official state sanctions although the state, especially in the colonial context, often turns a blind eye to the killing of indigenous peoples by groups of settler-colonizers that are geographically removed from the centre of power and over which it has little or no control. The massacre is limited in time, that is, it takes place over hours or days, not months and years, and is generally confined in one geographical place.[20]

A massacre is typically "a brutal but short event, aimed at intimidating the survivors," a quality important as we discuss the effects of terror below.[21] In addition, massacres are most often driven by the local context, especially in terms of longstanding grievances, but depend for their success (and for perpetrators' future freedom from punishment) upon "a higher authority to either approve or to turn a blind eye to the killings."[22] In such a context, as Alex J. Bellamy, a professor of peace and conflict studies, notes, perpetrators might credibly "calculate that the risk of potential punishment is outweighed by the utility of mass killing. This, in turn, suggests that they believe they can secure *sufficient legitimacy* and avoid punishment."[23] They can secure this sufficient legitimacy because a massacre, like a lynching, is often justified by reference to tradition or to the state of public opinion.

Obviously, race riots and massacres meet James Hawdon and John Ryan's definition of group violence, including both violence by a group and against a group. And we can easily describe a lynching as group violence when it entails the deaths of so many people—in fact, when it does, these three categories start to blend together. However, lynching most often manifested as the murder of a single individual, not a group of people. So how can we speak of lynching as group violence in the same sense when only one person has been targeted for murder?

To speak about violence perpetrated by or against a group, we must first develop an idea of what constitutes a group. This may seem like an exercise in the obvious, but a group, philosophically speaking, is not simply any collection of individuals, and we cannot explore the idea of group violence without setting some framework for identifying perpetrators and victims as part of some unique collectivity. Here it will be interesting to start with philosopher Larry May's nominalist account, which he first presented in his

1987 book *The Morality of Groups* and later developed further in his 2010 *Genocide: A Normative Account*. For May, groups are:

1. composed of individual human persons;
2. who are related to each other by organizational structure, solidarity, or common interests;
3. and who are identifiable both to the members, and to those who observe the members, by characteristic features.

Expanding upon this, May insists that "there must be an especially strong relationship among the members that allows for individuals to act together, namely, that allows for joint action" before we can consider the group as an agent. Too, for a recognized group to exist, there must be "in-group recognition as well as out-group recognition."[24] Or as he restates it later, "It is my contention that when both the perpetrators (out-group) *and* the victims (in-group) recognize the existence of a group that is being attacked, then this is sufficient for the group to 'exist' and be the subject of the sorts of harms that characterize genocide, namely, the intent to destroy the group."[25]

May's nominalism has attracted its share of criticism, perhaps most notably from philosopher Berel Lang, who asserts that May "explicitly denies not only intrinsic but even historical differences in the roles of different group structures, asserting that no particular groups are more important than any others."[26] For example, in some contexts, people may varyingly value their respective ethnic, racial, religious, or national identities above others; in fact, these various identities can come into conflict in certain situations, requiring that their relative ranking be reevaluated. For instance, individuals might choose to downgrade their linguistic identities in order to assimilate better in a new society, or they might upgrade their religious identities after experiencing, or seeing others experience, persecution for belonging to the same groups. Moreover, May's definition, according to Lang, ignores the fact that group identity often precedes, or at least heavily informs, individual identity, and thus "if individual identity is even minimally dependent on group relations, the latter would have a measure of reality that the individual alone does not."[27] The fact that language is only acquired in a group setting—and that language is typically acquired before our long-term memories start consolidating, and thus before we begin to possess a fully developed sense of individuality— speaks to how group identity can precede the individual. Finally, May's nominalism fails to account for the continual challenge any group identity faces, such as what literary theorist Patrick Colm Hogan terms "practical alienation" and "situational identification." Practical alienation constitutes a challenge to "the categorical identification on which we based our initial expectations of shared practical identity," such as encountering linguistic differences among those with whom we share a national bond.[28] Situational identification entails a disruption to categorical identity due to a smooth interaction with a person or persons from a definite out-group, which "leads us to question our difference from members of the out-group defined by that category.[29] In other words, group identity, when the group becomes sufficiently big, experiences perpetual challenges at the individual or subgroup level as to the ultimate relevance of that identity, which raises questions about May's third point regarding group identity, that members are easily identifiable to other members.

It should also be noted that May's nominalist account does not, in fact, account for the social reality (or unreality) of racial groups—something vitally important for any exploration of lynching as group violence. Sure, racial groups are composed of individuals, but those individuals are not necessarily united by any sort of organizational structure, sense of solidarity, or common interests. Moreover, as strange as it might sound, they are not necessarily, as May put it, "identifiable both to the members, and to those who observe the members, by characteristic features." Race, according to historian Ariela J. Gross, "was created and re-created every day through the workings of community institutions and individuals in daily life."[30] Nowhere does this fact shine most brightly than in antebellum freedom suits, in which a slave sued for freedom on the basis of being white, such as the successful freedom suit of Abby Guy in Arkansas in the 1850s. The physical attributes of Guy and others in her situation did not stop them from being enslaved; the group identity attributed to such individuals—that they were Black and thus slaves—was practically tautological, for would they be enslaved if they were not Black? Maybe the existence of a trail of paperwork helped to reinforce a belief that the object of purchase had sufficient African "blood" to be a slave, but paperwork alone was never enough to stifle the neurosis that was built up around issues of racial identity. As Gross writes,

> White Northerners may have been horrified by the idea of enslaved whites, but white Southerners were more concerned about the opposite possibility: What if people of African descent were lurking unknown in their midst, enjoying all the privileges of whiteness despite their hidden Black essence? Worse, what if race were

simply unknowable? How many people of "negro blood" might even now be passing as white, turning those who accepted them into fools?[31]

And as Mark Twain demonstrates in his 1892 novel *Pudd'nhead Wilson*, in which a slave woman exchanges her child with the child of her owner, one's racial identity (as defined by law and society) could remain unknown even to the individual. This creates a case in which we have legal definitions of group identity (in this case race) that violate May's nominalism, for that identity can remain unknown to both self and other. Despite such individuals successfully performing one particular racial identity for their entire lives, a slight change in circumstance can demand, according to the rules of society and law, a fundamental change in that person's station. Thus does philosopher Paul C. Taylor insist that races are social constructs, "things that we humans create in the transactions that define social life. Specifically, they are the probabilistically defined populations that result from the white supremacist determination to link appearance and ancestry to social location and life chances."[32] And race, as an oppressive construct, cannot be the property of any one individual but must be the property of the group, for oppression, according to philosopher David Livingstone Smith, is "an intrinsically political concept, because it pertains to the distribution and deployment of power among whole groups rather than between individuals. People are never oppressed as individuals. They're oppressed because of their real or imagined group identity (race, gender, ethnicity, religion, political affiliation, or any number of other things)."[33]

Philosopher Claudia Card also raises a challenge to May's nominalism by exploring the possibility that group identity can remain invisible to an individual from the dominant group until it is revealed through a challenge to prevailing hierarchies. As she writes:

> Suppose those who benefit rather than lose from a practice have less motivation to notice the benefit until it is jeopardized. Suppose also that those who are harmed have more motivation to notice and eventually reflect on sources. It would not be surprising, then, if men were not motivated to identify themselves in terms of their sex or gender except when there was a danger of being perceived or treated as women. It would be easier for most men not to be aware of their conditioning by sexual divisions of labor and compulsory heterosexuality, which, of course, limit their options, too, but in ways that tend to benefit their development or autonomy. Not noticing, one takes the status quo to be natural, normal, and defends it against attack.[34]

In other words, a group may not be aware of itself as a group until its status stands at risk, for status cannot be shared without diminishing its importance, its relevance. As James Hawdon writes, "The inexpansible nature of status makes preserving the group's integrity paramount; thus, efforts to clearly mark and protect group boundaries intensify. To fail to do so risks diluting the importance of membership; it risks inflation. Because status is expansible, if others gain it, those with it lose it. Thus, those of higher status fight to maintain the status hierarchy that provides them with privileges."[35] This will tie in directly to our application of René Girard's mimetic theory to the phenomenon of lynching in chapter 5; for the moment, it will suffice to cite theologian Wolfgang Palaver's observation that "the disappearance of difference—physical or metaphysical—results in an increase in the frequency and intensity of conflict between the groups. Conflicts between equals have the greatest risk of turning violent, because the social limitations that normally prevent or channel mimetic desire are missing."[36]

In the sense that it produces the possibility of violence, group identity can be regarded as conflictual and dialectic. A group consciousness emerges among a people through a shared sense of oppression or persecution, and their resistance to that, in turn, causes the advantaged group to feel its status jeopardized, thus producing a shared group identity as they endeavor to maintain traditional privileges. In the American context, Blackness is defined against whiteness as much as whiteness is defined against Blackness. Or as historian Patrick Wolfe puts it, race "is a process, not an ontology, its varying modalities so many dialectical symptoms of the ever-shifting hegemonic balance between those with a will to colonise and those with a will to be free, severally racialised in relation to each other."[37]

Group identity exists dialectically, and acts of violence may well be part of that dialect. But can we speak of lynching as an act of group violence in both senses that Hawdon and Ryan specify—violence both by a group and against a group? Author Jan Voogd notes the similarities between large-scale riots and lynchings, writing, "Both lynching mobs and rioting mobs used precipitating events as excuses to try to justify their violence, and in both cases these excuses were usually an alleged crime of social trespass of some sort of black individual." However, he differentiates between them in terms of their intended targets: "The direct target of a lynching was the individual(s), and the community was targeted indirectly. By contrast, a riot targeted the community directly."[38] But this distinction assumes that the mob makes such a distinction itself. According to the philosopher Arne Johan Vetlesen, "There is no identity to be had for the single individual apart from that bestowed and secured by a given community and, in times of upheaval and conflict, endangered by some given other community."[39] And Lang argues that even when an act of violence is directed toward a specific individual, we can still see that act as an example of group violence if said individual "is attacked not for anything he himself is or does, but for his relation to a group, a relation over which he has no control; the reason for the attack is not personal interest, gain, or inclination, but the principle that membership in the group itself suffices to exclude him from the domain of humanity."[40]

And indeed, we will follow Lang's line of argument, for lynching often did not simply entail the murder of an individual—rather, it encompassed a range of activities that very specifically targeted Black communities as a whole. As the journalist Ziya Us Salam observes regarding lynching in twenty-first-century India, "It strikes at the very identity of the community. It is far more demoralizing than the traditional communal violence, but serves the same purpose as riots did in the years gone by: to engender a climate of distrust and fear."[41] To say that a lynching was accomplished the moment the victim stopped breathing constitutes a tremendous distortion of the historical record. Let us turn to a few examples.

On March 11, 1894, a group of African Americans were traveling from the community of Marche back to their homes in nearby Little Rock when "they found the decayed body of a mulatto woman probably about 30 years of age suspended from the limb of a tree." Upon closer inspection, the woman seemed to have been dead for several days, and on her chest was a placard bearing the words, "If anybody cuts this body down they will share the same fate." As the *Arkansas Gazette* reported, "The woman is supposed to have been lynched, but when, by whom, and for what reason no one is able to state."[42]

That fact can make this particular murder perhaps a greater source of terror than a more public lynching. After all, lynchings were publicly justified as a response to particular misdeeds—murder, rape, theft, and so forth—and although the reality was that lynch mobs could attack individuals not associated with the crime at all, or that sometimes people were lynched to eliminate competition rather than serve the cause of justice, at least the reference to criminality gave those in the targeted communities a baseline of expected behavior. In other words, the mob meant lynching to be pedagogical, to be instructive to those witnessing it, or even simply reading about it or hearing about it in the days and years to come. But what "lesson" can this 1894 lynching provide? The identity of the woman, the identity of the perpetrators, the reason for the murder—all of these remain unknown. Were the victim a man, certain assumptions might be made about whom he wronged or "outraged," but the fact that it was a dead woman at the end of the rope makes it more difficult to relate to the typical motivations for lynching. So all that remains is the terrible awareness that maybe nothing at all can prevent the mob or posse from showing up at your door, protected by absolute impunity; that such a murder can occur for no good reason whatsoever but, rather, strikes like lightning from a clear blue sky. That is the nature of terror. And this lesson is for everybody.

More often, the mob was not so oblique about its threat to the entire Black community. On the night of Saturday, December 18, 1909, a Black man named George Bailey reportedly entered a saloon near the Prairie County town of Biscoe in southeastern Arkansas, where he asked bartender Matt Todd for a gallon of whiskey on credit. Todd "told the negro that he would have to see the proprietor of the place" about the request, after which Bailey went outside and shot at Todd through the window, hitting him in the arm and "shattering the bone just below the elbow." Bailey escaped but was arrested the next day and brought to the jail at nearby De Valls Bluff. According to the *Arkansas Gazette*, "public feeling" against Black people had already been "greatly aroused" the previous week after an African American broke into a boxcar and "made a murderous attack upon a sleeping white man, nearly cutting the latters [*sic*] throat in an attempt to rob him." In fact, a mob had been gathered to lynch this unnamed person, "but cooler counsel prevailed."[43]

Bailey's alleged assault, however, "stirred up new feeling" among those who "evidently decided that they would take no chances on having their plans thwarted again." A lynch mob broke into the jail that Sunday evening and fired into Bailey's body fifteen times. Despite all of this shooting, the *Gazette* reported, somewhat incredulously, that the murder of Bailey "was accomplished so quietly that persons sleeping a block away were not awakened." The sheriff was even said to have had "no intimation of the affair" until he opened up the jail and discovered the body.[44]

But Bailey's murder was not just the occasion to exact vengeance upon an individual miscreant. After the murder, rumors circulated "that the negroes had held secret meetings during the day." In response to these rumors, "bands of armed white citizens patrolled the streets ... firing occasional shots by way of warning. Rope nooses were placed over the doors of negro residences." In other words, a campaign of terror was unleashed—and it apparently worked. As the *Gazette* noted: "The blacks, if they had any intentions of starting trouble, appear to have been awed by these measures. Hardly a negro is to be seen upon the streets tonight. Many of them left town during the day. Others have disappeared and are supposed to be hiding in the nearby country. It is not believed that there will be further trouble."[45]

In 1916, when an armed posse lynched Will Warren in rural Garland County in the Ouachita Mountains of western Arkansas, they did not confine themselves to outrages upon his body alone. Reports are vague on the exact nature of Warren's alleged crime, with the *Hot Springs New Era* explaining that the man "became engaged in a quarrel with some white boys," which was then "taken up by the parents of the boys." During the course of this conflict, Warren apparently locked himself in his house, but the armed posse fired through the doors and windows to kill him. However, the feelings of the mob spilled over onto the predominantly Black settlement, located between the communities of Buckville and Cedar Glades, where Warren lived. As the *Arkansas Gazette* reported, Warren "was one of the leading negroes at the settlement. His alleged insult toward the white boys caused a general ill feeling against the settlement and in an attempt to 'get even' the white men burned the negro church after killing Warren and burning his house."[46]

When the activist organization Equal Justice Initiative (EJI) of Montgomery, Alabama, released the first edition of their report *Lynching in America: Confronting the Legacy of Racial Terror*, in 2015, they described lynching as "violent and public acts of torture that traumatized Black people throughout the country," acts that were "largely tolerated by state and federal officials."[47] The terminology employed by EJI, "terror lynchings," is not one broadly accepted by scholars, and their description of lynching as an explicitly public activity ignores the fact that many such murders were often perpetrated quietly, in the dead of night, by a small, private mob, and that the display of the body or public performance of the murder was not necessary to inspire terror in the Black population at large. Often, disappearances could be just as frightening. After all, Emmett Till's body was never meant to be found, and many local African Americans—and whites—spoke in 1955 of the Tallahatchie River, where his corpse was located, as being full of Black bodies that had been dumped there discreetly.

However, EJI's approach does reveal a reality about lynching that earlier scholarly definitions often overlooked, those that emphasized the support of the community or the pretext of service to tradition. Such an emphasis may function within a more capacious definition of lynching, one that attempts to encompass all its manifestations, from frontier justice to racial terror. But white-on-Black lynching had the support only of the white community and was perpetrated on the pretext of very specific traditions of segregation and oppression. What can we say about the effect upon the Black community, especially when the act of lynching exceeded the "punishment" of the individual targeted? According to the EJI report, "The practice of terrorizing an entire African American community after lynching one alleged 'wrongdoer' demonstrates that Southern lynching during this era was not to attain 'popular justice' or retaliation for crime. Rather, these lynchings were designed for broad impact—to send a message of domination, to instill fear, and sometimes to drive African Americans from the community altogether."[48] These lynchings, moreover, constituted but part of a broader tapestry of objective, or structural, violence; this will be explored more fully in chapter 2, but it will be sufficient for now to note that this entailed the use of terrorism "to relegate African Americans to a state of second-class citizenship and economic disadvantage that would last for generations after emancipation and create far-reaching consequences."[49]

How does terror serve the function of relegating whole Black populations to second-class status? According to anthropologists Andrew Strathern and Pamela J. Stewart, terror is

> based on an interlocking feedback between memory and anticipation, the same nexus that makes possible continuity in human interaction generally. Here, however, the feedback is based on a sense of rupture. Terror consists precisely in intrusions into expectations about security, making moot the mundane processes on which social life otherwise depends. Repeated ruptures shift people's perceptions and render them progressively more anxious and vulnerable to disturbance.[50]

For example, an abused child may flinch at the raising of a hand or clenching of a fist precisely because he does not know whether a strike is forthcoming; the pattern of abuse has ruptured that feedback between memory and anticipation. A slap, a hit, may be possible at any moment, and so one needs to observe the signs constantly and never become comfortable. Many abusers revel in their ability to strike terror in their charges with just the slightest twitch of a hand.[51] Terror, according to Strathern and Stewart, does not merely rest upon the initial act of violence; "it rests also on the great multiplication of reactions to these acts and the fears that these acts arouse in people's imaginations."[52] Or as anthropologist Veena Das writes:

> It is not only violence experienced on one's body in these cases but also the sense that one's access to context is lost that constitutes a sense of being violated. The fragility of the social becomes embedded in a temporality of anticipation since one ceases to trust that context is in place. The effect produced on the registers of the virtual and the potential, of fear that is real but not necessarily actualized in events, comes to constitute the ecology of fear in everyday life. Potentiality here does not have the sense of something that is waiting at the door of reality to make an appearance as it were, but rather as that which is already present.[53]

For Claudia Card, a form of terrorism like lynching, in mirroring how abuse functions, "creates an *atmosphere of grave uncertainty and insecurity* in the face of what could be imminent danger. Uncertainty and insecurity can make fears *reasonable*."[54] After all, there was no one thing, one specific act, for which mobs lynched people. Mobs often justified their actions by reference to the "outrage" perpetrated upon a white woman, by which they meant rape, but mobs just as easily lynched men for carrying out acknowledged consensual relationships, as we will explore in chapter 5.

Moreover, a misunderstood word could be taken as an insult, an act of self-defense could be interpreted as "insolence" or a potential "uprising," or a man walking home at night could be mistaken for the criminal everyone is seeking. All of this served to create a collective rupture in the feedback loop between memory and anticipation, a rupture that facilitated the intimidation of whole Black communities. Vinikas emphasizes this point when he writes, "The southern strain of mob murder was not just antilegal, it was often acausal as well. That was the essence of its terror. To argue that a southern lynching was predictable—the logical outcome of perceived transgression—is to miss the essential didactic message of the phenomenon in maintaining white supremacy."[55] This is what makes terror such a potent tool in the hands of the ruling castes and classes, and is why terror has often been the first and last resort of regimes seeking to sideline any challenge to their rule. As historian Thomas C. Wright observes, "The intent of terrorism by the state is to eliminate some or all of the people who are considered actual or potential enemies of the regime, and to marginalize those not eliminated through the fear that terrorism instills."[56] But the fear fostered by the regular rupture inflicted by regimes of terror exists at an extreme, according to Card: "It tends to be incapacitating, makes us less able to resist, focuses our energies non-productively, interferes with the ability to think and plan. In these ways it undermines competence."[57]

Probably the most notorious use of lynching as a means to threaten the entire Black community occurred on May 4, 1927, in Little Rock. And the person whom the mob lynched likely had nothing whatsoever to do with any crime committed.

On April 30, the body of an eleven-year-old white

girl, Floella McDonald, was found in the belfry of First Presbyterian Church in downtown Little Rock by the church's Black janitor, Frank Dixon. Police immediately began questioning Dixon, as well as his teenage son Lonnie, grilling them for hours, in addition to rounding up some of their known associates. The following day, the police announced that they had an oral confession to the murder from Lonnie, though, as historian Stephanie Harp notes, this was obtained only "after between sixteen and twenty-four hours of questioning, most of it endured while standing and without food or legal counsel."[58] According to this confession, Lonnie lured the young Floella into the belfry with a promise of gifts, raped her, and then hit her on the head with a brick; however, he repudiated his confession the next day, perhaps returning to his senses after a respite from the relentless interrogation.

Once news was released that Lonnie had confessed, a mob numbering in the thousands formed outside city hall, demanding the blood of both Dixons, but the police chief managed to sneak the two away in separate cars for safekeeping in separate jails far from Little Rock. The mob also broke into the state penitentiary to search for the Dixons but, when they heard that the father and son had been successfully spirited away from Little Rock, broke up to drive to nearby communities in an attempt to search their jails. The mob spirit generated by the police investigation into Floella McDonald's death would serve as the catalyst for the lynching of a man wholly unconnected to this affair, a man named John Carter.

What exactly happened on the morning of May 4, 1927, will likely never be known. All that is known of the precipitating affair is that two white women, Mrs. B. E. Stewart and her daughter Glennie, were driving a wagon into Little Rock from southwest of the city when they encountered an African American man walking along the road. As Harp writes:

> Greatly varying reports said that he asked them the location of a bridge, or whether they were going to town, or if they had any whiskey; that he ran and caught the wagon, jumped in, and grabbed the reins; that either he threatened to kill the women or he beat them with an iron bar; that Glennie fought back with a whip, that he knocked both of them out of the wagon or that they fell or jumped, and that Mrs. Stewart broke her arm; that he threw rocks at them, or chased one or both, and caught up with Glennie—or her mother—and attacked with a tree limb, and beat the mother unconscious.[59]

And those are just the variations of the story within the white-owned press; a body of oral history from Little Rock's Black community paints an even more diverse picture, often of a man attempting to help the women regain the control of their cart. Either way, though, a Black man was found in the presence of screaming white women and fled. Word spread. The sheriff showed up with four carloads of deputies to begin the search, and soon some fifteen hundred volunteers from Little Rock were beating the bushes in search of their prey.

Eventually, the mob captured a man later identified as John Carter and sent for Glennie Stewart to identify him. When she did, the "volunteers" seized Carter, taking him from the officers assembled there, and hanged him from a telephone pole for about two minutes before firing about two hundred or three hundred shots into his body.

The crowd dispersed at the urging of the sheriff (who later claimed he arrived after the deed was done, although witnesses placed him there the entire time) but later reassembled and voted to take the body into Little Rock and burn it there. The procession of cars dragged Carter's body, unchallenged, through the main thoroughfares of Little Rock—even driving by the county courthouse, city hall, and police headquarters—before finally stopping at the intersection of Ninth and Broadway in what was then the heart of the Black business district, home to the national headquarters of the Mosaic Templars of America, a Black fraternal organization. "There," Harp writes, "they placed Carter's body at the intersection of two streetcar lines, doused it with gasoline, and set it on fire, using pews from nearby Bethel African Methodist Episcopal (AME) Church, Little Rock's largest African American church."[60] The mob, estimated at between four thousand and seven thousand, went riot for hours until the National Guard was called out to restore order. While all of this was going on, most of the police were apparently hiding in the basement of their headquarters, although some sources reported seeing officers mingling with the mob without attempting to stop the violence at all.[61] In many stories of lynching, the role of the police is ambiguous—often does a guard or deputy claim, after the fact, to have been overpowered by a mob; often does a sheriff disappear as rumors of impending violence hit the air; often do the collective law enforcement agencies completely fail to investigate a lynching at all. But it would be a mistake to write this off as the aggregate result of bad actors; as political scientist Santana Khanikar observes, a focus upon corrupt or even evil individual police personnel means that "the institutional structures and ideologies of the organization are not questioned."[62]

As we will discuss in chapter 3, the site chosen for a lynching often bears significance for the mob. In this case, the mob killed Carter near where he was found but then decided to extend the narrative, to showcase the body and its destruction for a particular audience—the city's most successful African Americans. Why? They were not responsible for Carter's actions in any way, at least objectively. However, mob violence operates under a different dynamic, namely what Vetlesen calls "the logic of generic attribution," which reduces each individual to a member of a group and thus holds the group responsible for the actions of the individual. As he explains:

> What generic attribution does is to *collectivize agency* and its various properties and dimensions, be they moral, legal, or spatiotemporal.... When human agency is thoroughly collectivized, in-group differences evaporate and inter-group differences are polarized in the extreme. Once collectivized, human agency is conceived in such a way that the individual is compelled to answer for everything "his" group does, has done, or is said to be about to do; conversely, the group is made to answer for everything a single individual member of it has done, does, or is said to contemplate doing.... The guilt of one group and the victimhood of the other are both eternalized. ... Such eternalization of victimhood goes hand in hand with the *essentialization* of identity that is a salient feature of genocidal ideologies.[63]

The neighborhood of West Ninth Street in Little Rock was the center of Black middle-class life, complete with entertainment venues, fraternal organizations, law offices, and more.[64] Therefore, in many ways, it compounded the insult to burn John Carter's body there, to signify a lack of recognition of the class differences between this man and those who lived and labored at West Ninth.

While Carter's body was taken to a Black neighborhood for ritual degradation, to serve as a warning to all African Americans, other mobs had previously conducted, with great deliberation, lynchings in Black neighborhoods, even if the victim had no connection with the people who lived there. A noteworthy case of this, which occurred in the community of Stuttgart in 1916, will be explored further in chapter 3, but that same year, a man named Frank Dodd was lynched in DeWitt in southeastern Arkansas, in a manner that speaks of Vetlesen's "logic of generic attribution." According to the *Arkansas Gazette*, Dodd encountered two white women riding a wagon to DeWitt and asked for a ride. Once installed in the wagon, he "began to talk insultingly" to one of the women and refused their demands that he leave until a local farmer, John Lacotts, succeeded in driving him off. However, Dodd "followed until Lacotts had gone and then continued to annoy the young women." According to the *Arkansas Democrat*, however, Dodd stood accused of "attempting to assault" a single woman driving alone and following her for half a mile "before her cries attracted attention of persons, who frightened the negro." Dodd was swiftly arrested and jailed in DeWitt, but as stories spread about the incident, "the officers hid the negro because of fear of mob violence." Thinking that the community had calmed down enough, the officers returned Dodd to the jail, but they had apparently been watched, for a mob quickly formed and forced the jailer at gunpoint to deliver Dodd to them. As the *Gazette* reported, "The negro was taken quietly to the negro section of town and hanged to a tree. Several dozen bullets were fired into the body, but few white residents were aroused by the noise. . . . Negroes in town were greatly excited this morning, but the town was quiet tonight."[65]

Let us return to the thirteen lynched in St. Charles. Although the *Arkansas Gazette*, in its reporting on the affair, was vague about the questions of where, when, how, and why the violence occurred, the newspaper rather interestingly made sure to list every Black victim by name: Abe Bailey, Mack Baldwin, Will Baldwin, Garrett Flood, Randall Flood, Aaron Hinton, Will Madison, Charley Smith, Jim Smith, Perry Carter, Kellis Johnson, Henry Griffin, and Walker Griffin. This might give the impression that it was only individuals who were sought out for extermination. But notice how many of those men share last names: Baldwin, Flood, Smith, and Griffin. Now, it is no longer simply individuals who are the targets of violence but, instead, possible families, and a family would meet any definition of a group. But even if the *Gazette* wanted to emphasize in its reporting that only individuals were targeted, a later editorial on the subject, once the shooting had subsided, should serve to erase all doubt as to the nature of the violence employed in this corner of southeastern Arkansas:

> For the sake of the good name of the state of Arkansas, let us hope that the race war between whites and blacks in Arkansas county is at an end.
>
> The last reports received said that thirteen negroes had been killed since the trouble began, but it was thought that peace had been restored.
>
> The negroes threw down the gauntlet to the authorities and the whites promptly took it up. Wherever the negroes take the position that

they won't submit to arrest, that their weight of numbers gives them the right or the power to do as they please, a conflict between the two races is inevitable.

But it should be remembered that a race war in which thirteen men are killed on one side is a perfect feast for the big newspapers all over the United States, especially for certain ones north of the Mason and Dixon line that seem to delight to feature something that paints Southern life in a bad way.[66]

The "negroes threw down the gauntlet" and the whites "took it up," creating "a conflict between the two races." The editorial even dispenses with the usual rhetoric about specific "bad negroes" and, instead, assumes a wholly dualistic worldview that essentializes the two groups and presumes an ongoing relationship of conflict between them. The editorial writer even fails to appreciate the irony of African Americans believing that "their weight of numbers gives them the right or the power to do as they please" in the face of reporting about how a white mob kidnapped five Black men from a jail where they had been securely held, unarmed, and subsequently butchered them without fear of arrest themselves. But then, as we have seen, that sense of mob impunity was a standard feature of every lynching, whether it was ravenous posses roaming the woods around St. Charles or a smaller group of vigilantes quietly murdering a young woman in the dead of night and leaving her body to hang and rot as a warning to all.

2

STRUCTURE

But the truth is that if division and violence define war, the world has always been at war and always will be . . .

—Simone de Beauvoir, *The Ethics of Ambiguity*[1]

ON MAY 17, 1909, Governor George Washington Donaghey of Arkansas signed into law Act 258, titled "An Act to Prevent Mob Violence or Lynching within the State of Arkansas." Although it was occasionally described in the newspapers of the era as an anti-lynching law, Act 258 was nothing of the kind. Instead, it required that, "whenever the crime of rape, attempt to commit rape, murder or any other crime, calculated to arouse the passions of the people to an extent that the sheriff of the county believes that mob violence will be committed," the sheriff was to notify the district or circuit judge in order to request "a special term of court in order that the person or persons charged with such crime or crimes may be brought to immediate trial." If the judge in question found that "the apprehensions and belief of the sheriff are well founded," it was his responsibility to arrange for an immediate trial, to take place in no fewer than ten days from the receipt of such notice. If the circuit judge was ill or absent, then the lawyers practicing in his circuit could elect a special judge to perform the necessary duties for this particular trial. Citizens numbering at least seven could, in the face of the sheriff's refusal to issue such a request to the local judge, demand that he do so in writing, and if he then failed to do his duty, said sheriff could be deemed guilty of a misdemeanor and fined between $200 and $1,000. Of course, there was no such fine for any sheriff who let his prisoner be taken by the mob, nor any mechanism established for better prosecuting members of any lynch mob. All this bill did was expedite a trial during the narrow time frame when the atmosphere of mob justice still prevailed. This was no anti-lynching law.[2]

Act 258 was originally written by Father John Michael Lucey of Pine Bluff and was introduced in the Arkansas Senate on January 25, 1909, by Senator Hardin K. Toney. Lucey, who was described by the *Arkansas Gazette* rather sympathetically as "one of the best known of the Catholic clergy of the South, and an ex-Confederate soldier," appeared before the Judiciary Committee the following month to speak up for his bill. One member of the committee did note that calling a grand jury, indicting a person, and then holding a trial while local sentiment was still inflamed seemed a questionable legal practice, while another member, apparently less sympathetic to the right of those on trial, observed that nothing "could be enacted into law constitutionally that would prevent a defendant in a criminal proceeding from taking a change of venue to another part of the judicial district."[3]

Lucey wrote to the *Gazette* a few days later to defend his bill against the first charge, not by defending the ability of a circuit court to hold a genuinely fair trial so close in time to the alleged criminal deed, but instead by insisting that the immediate enaction of legal measures would be the best means to prevent a lynching: "Is there a better chance for the ends of justice to be served by a mob, who will decide the whole matter in a few hours, than by a court of justice that would be allowed ten days, with all the forms of Grand Jury, Petit Jury, lawyers for defense and for prosecution, and a learned judge presiding?" He also implied that the (white) citizenry only performed lynchings due to the perceived necessity of action and found no pleasure in the deed at all: "On the contrary, it is as repulsive a piece of business as can be conceived for men of high character to imbrue their hands in the blood of a negro brute. They are impelled to do this ugly work solely because there is no other means at hand of meting out proper justice. They would be rejoiced if the judiciary of the state would relieve them of the fearful alternative."[4]

To back up his point, Lucey referenced a recent case in which, he claimed, a lynching was averted in the Arkansas community of Hampton by promise of a speedy trial. The previous December, two African Americans, brothers Henry and Wilson Pickett, had fled Calhoun County in south central Arkansas following the murder of local planter Charles Abbott and the shooting of his brother, county treasurer F. M. Abbott. The Pickett brothers were arrested in Monroe, Louisiana, in early 1909 and returned to Arkansas, but authorities had to spirit them away from Hampton on January 20, 1909, after a mob of some hundred people gathered due to rumors (later proven true) that the defense attorney was seeking a change of venue. The Pickett brothers were scheduled to go on trial on March 29 in El Dorado, located in neighboring Union County, which abuts the Louisiana state line. However, on the day of the trial, a mob of seventy-five men left Hampton for El Dorado, intending to storm the jail and lynch the brothers. Local authorities in El Dorado, hearing of the coming mob, contacted Governor Donaghey, and the governor dispatched twenty members of the state guard to the city. The troops were posted around the jail, and the mob lingered until the evening before returning home, not willing to take a chance against trained troops. (Rumors that the pair were lynched, however, did make it into the *Arkansas Gazette*.) A few days later, the Pickett brothers were put on trial and sentenced to twenty-one years in the state penitentiary.[5] For Lucey to claim that this sequence of events justified his faith in expedited trials was a stretch, to say the least.

The Lucey bill passed the Senate on April 8, 1909; it passed the House on May 12 by a vote of 54 to 24 and went to the governor's desk for his signature.[6] On the same day the bill passed the House, the *Arkansas Gazette* reported that one Abe Green, "a negro, 35 years of age," had narrowly escaped a lynching. Green had been arrested on May 10 in the community of Formosa, located in north central Arkansas, "on a charge of committing an assault upon the 13-year-old daughter of a prominent farmer in that section." He was subsequently positively identified by the reported victim, Ura Webb, daughter of J. M. Webb, and taken to Clinton, the county seat. Given that the people of Formosa "were greatly aroused," officers removed Green to the jail in Marshall, located in Searcy County, two counties to the west, in order to prevent a lynching. Sure enough, despite being apprised of Green's relocation, several residents of Formosa travelled to Clinton "to make an investigation," and the *Gazette* reported: "There is no doubt that Green would have been lynched if he had been kept in the jail" at Clinton. The initial report ended thusly: "Efforts are being made to get into communication with Judge B. B. Hudgins and it is probable that a special term of court will be held."

Green went on trial in early June, and his jury debated forty minutes before sentencing him to die by hanging on July 9.[7] However, on appeal, the Arkansas Supreme Court issued a writ of error and, just days before the scheduled hanging, granted a stay of execution as they heard his appeal. In October, the court reduced his sentence to twenty-one years in prison, ruling that "the facts did not warrant a conviction on any charge more serious than attempted criminal assault."[8]

Both the Pickett and the Green cases demonstrate that authorities had the means to prevent lynchings without promising expedited trials, contrary to Lucey's assertions. In Green's case, the removal of the suspect from the area where the alleged crime was committed seems to have played a significant role. In the Pickett case, a relocation combined with a show of state authority helped to preserve the life, if not the liberty, of the defendant.

But Lucey's 1909 bill was, arguably, intended less to prevent lynchings than it was to prevent more radical legislation, such as that introduced into the Arkansas General Assembly two years prior by State Senator Kie Oldham of Pulaski County. Senator Oldham described his as a "drastic bill" when he introduced it on January 22, 1907, and the *Arkansas Gazette*, the state's largest newspaper, agreed with the description. The bill required that any sheriff or other law enforcement officer, "having in his possession a man charged with a crime, and against whom the sentiment of the community is inflamed," protect said person from the mob or face, at minimum, a $1,000 fine and six-month sentence in the state penitentiary—although an exemption was made in cases where said officer was wounded. But the potential responsibility extended also to members of the general public, for the bill provided officers the right to summon help to defend prisoners and, likewise, applied the same potential penalties to those individuals. Oldham had also offered a bill earlier that session requiring expedited trials, to take place within ten days, for those persons "against whom the wrath of any community was aroused." During the subsequent debate in the Arkansas Senate Judiciary Committee of this measure to suppress mob violence, Oldham reiterated that his bill was indeed "drastic" but asked the committee "whether we had rather have this kind of legislation or lynchings in Arkansas." In response, Senator Howard Robb of Desha County (located in southeastern Arkansas and described by the *Gazette* as "one of those 'black' counties") insisted that "while he had never participated in a mob or advocated mob law, yet there were instances in which it was to be condoned when the fair women of the commonwealth were made the victims of a black brute's fiendish desire."[9]

The Judiciary Committee advanced Oldham's bill to expedite trials for those "against whom the community is aroused," which required a sheriff or other official in charge of such a prisoner to notify the circuit court judge, who would then be authorized to convene a special session.[10] This bill was ultimately defeated in the Arkansas House of Representatives on the charge "that it was revolutionary and would place the sheriff or any county in an attitude of dictating to the judiciary."[11] However, prior to the bill's defeat, Father Lucey wrote the *Gazette* to endorse the first of Oldham's two bills, the one demanding expedited trials as a means of reducing mob violence, while insisting that, regarding the second bill, "I am not yet qualified to pass judgment upon it, not having weighed the matter as I would like." He went on to state (and it is worth quoting at length):

> I sympathize very deeply with Senator Robb and a few others who may oppose the bill to

which I refer, but I cannot agree with them that there will arise instances in which lynching is justifiable. An instance may arise when it will be allowable to rise up against the government, but that is revolution. There is no instance where it is contemplated that men shall willfully and overtly break a law of the land and still remain immune under the law. It is a matter of great surprise that a man can take his place as a lawmaker in a legislative chamber in soberness and sincerity while believing in his heart that men are not obliged to obey any laws there enacted. Such sentiments might possibly be entertained outside of a legislature, but they should not be tolerated within it.

For the life of me I cannot understand what our civil government is for if not to afford citizens security of home and protection in the ordinary pursuits of life. The state of Arkansas makes these promises to her citizens and yet when the Supreme moment arrives when a horrible monster invades the home and deflowers its fairest possessions, the civil government stands listlessly by and declares that it should do nothing. There is nothing in the world that is so grateful to a family in dire distress as to know that they have the fullest sympathy of friends and neighbors. Why should they not also have the fullest sympathy of that paternal government which receives their taxes and talks so glibly when elections are at hand and has so many judges and officers in high places. If the people fully knew that they had the fullest sympathy of the civil government in their hour of terrible sorrow and that the officers of that government would make every sacrifice that any human power could make to vindicate justice and afford relief, they would apply to that government as readily as they now apply to friends and neighbors and they would not imbrue their hands and involve their dearest friends in the sinful and gross procedure of barbarous times and savage peoples, that of burning at the stake or hanging a human creature.[12]

The reader will notice that Lucey, despite his plea for legal protections covering those who would otherwise be lynched, nonetheless depicts potential victims of lynching in the exact same manner as do those who support lethal vigilantism. Or as rhetorician Ersula J. Ore has written, "Such discourse rhetorically situating lynchings as a consequence of black debauchery worked to combat accusations of white barbarity by casting blacks as morally unfit for society."[13] Lucey describes a potential victim of lynching as "a horrible monster" who "invades the home and deflowers its fairest possessions," evoking the "Black beast rapist" myth used to justify so many lynchings. His plea of security for citizens does not extend to the potential victims of lynching because he does not conceive them as citizens. Instead, it is those who experience such home invasions at the hands of a "horrible monster" who are accorded the "fullest sympathy" of the government to whom they pay taxes. Moreover, this "paternal government" is the best authority to "vindicate justice and afford relief," and if people could accept that, then they would not need to resort to lynching, because the government would, essentially, take the burden upon themselves to avenge its suffering citizens.

Lucey, apparently, cannot imagine—or does not

intend—such a government affording the potential lynching victim an adequate defense and, horror of horrors, even finding him innocent based upon the evidence at hand. As historian Michael J. Pfeifer has written, legislators across the nation "reshaped the death penalty in the early twentieth century to make capital punishment more efficient and more racial, achieving a compromise between the observations of legal forms long emphasized by due process advocates and the lethal, ritualized retribution long sought by rough justice supporters."[14] Moreover, Lucey's bill and the rhetoric he employed to defend it essentially conceded that the "passions" of the people were justified when inflamed in response to certain crimes. This rhetoric applies to the "negro," to the "horrible monster," what literary theorist Patrick Colm Hogan has dubbed an "attribution of absolute moral culpability," one that frees the citizenry to respond with what butchery it will. That is, the first act of violence "was a free and purely immoral choice, while the response was, in some sense, not free but compelled by the initiating act. Thus, the apparent immorality of the response does not taint the group responding, but accrues to the immorality of the initiating act."[15] Or as researcher Sonja Schillings states, "Whoever claims legitimate violence marks something as worthy of protection— say, a community—and simultaneously formulates the expectation that even those who are (potentially) the target of violence accept this community's basic worthiness of protection. In this sense, an act of legitimate violence does not begin but ends the conflict; it simply reacts to a violent attack that transgresses a boundary and everything 'behind' it."[16]

Four lynchings were recorded in Arkansas in the year 1909—two of them occurring in the weeks following the passage of Act 258. The first victim, Lovett Davis, was arrested in Pine Bluff for breaking into the home of Knowlton Padgett and choking his sixteen-year-old niece, Amy Holmes, on the morning of May 23. Likely to prevent a lynching, the officers responding to the assault did not circulate the story to the press until the suspect had been captured, and upon capture, Davis "admitted choking the girl, but says that he did not attempt to assault her: that he had entered the house for the purpose of robbing it and that when she awoke he choked her to prevent her from giving the alarm."[17]

The events of the following day would seem to prove wrong Lucey's assertion that a community promised the speedy trial of a "negro brute" would allow state justice to take its course. Worried that a lynching was likely, Sheriff C. M. Philpot stood guard around the jail with a number of deputies and other officers, and at midnight, when a mob of some two hundred people showed up, "drew his revolver and declared that the man who attempted to enter the jail would die." This held the mob in check for a few minutes before its leaders rushed the sheriff and forced their way into the jail. Hearing of this, the local circuit judge, A. B. Grace, made his way to the jail and implored the mob to cease its actions, telling them, "If you will go home and let the negro remain in jail I will order a special Grand Jury at once, and the case will go to trial at the earliest possible moment," all in accordance with Act 258. He even threatened the mob with sanction, insisting that he would work to bring them to justice if they lynched Davis, but the mob disregarded him and dragged the prisoner from the jail. They hanged Davis at the corner of Second and Main streets in downtown Pine Bluff, "just in front of the Progress clothing store," but on their first attempt, the rope broke, and Davis, "yet alive struck the ground with a thud that made the spectators shudder with horror." So members of the mob adjusted the noose and made a second, more successful attempt at the hanging. As the *Arkansas Gazette* reported, "At the corner where the lynching took place a cluster of 500 incandescent electric lights have bene [*sic*] arranged for the Arkansas Travelers convention next month. When the mob gathered these, in common with all others in the city, were dark, but as the body of the negro swung into space the second time, and it was certain that the rope would hold, these 500 lights flashed out, the current turned on in some mysterious manner, the glare of the hundreds of bulbs added ghastliness to the scene."[18]

As promised, Judge Grace did convene a grand jury following the lynching, and at the coroner's inquest, Sheriff Philpot admitted to recognizing several members of the mob, none of whom wore any sort of mask. As the *Arkansas Democrat* reported, however, public sentiment greatly favored the lynching party, "and it is not thought that they will be convicted even if indicted."[19] Even in his charge to the grand jury, insisting that "the law must reign supreme," Grace echoed the rhetoric of Lucey as to the inherently criminal nature of African Americans, saying, "The women of today don't fear murder, but the white women of the south live in a constant fear of terror that some black brute might attack them. The crime of assault is not a white man's vice. It seems to be principally among the illiterate negroes." He later added, "The white man's blood boils when the honor of our women is attacked."[20] Nothing ultimately appears to have come from the grand jury investigation.

The promise of an expedited trial failed to stop the lynching of Lovett Davis, and the next lynching to follow the passage of Act 258 did not even target the person who allegedly perpetrated the precipitating criminal act. The matter started in late May 1909 when Bud Harper, a white farmer living near Portland in southern Arkansas, killed a dog belonging to a Black man, Sam Blakely. According to reports, Sam and his brother, Joe, went to Harper's house to confront him over the matter, and while Joe held a gun on Harper, Sam beat the farmer repeatedly. Deputy Sheriff Walter Cain went to Sam's house to arrest the two men but, after forcing open the door, was immediately shot and killed. Sam Blakely, the apparent culprit, hopped a northbound train and eventually ended up in Mississippi before being captured and returned to Arkansas the following month (his exact fate remains unclear). Meanwhile, Joe Blakely was arrested as an accessory to the murder and ended up lynched on May 29, although not for anything to do with the murder of Deputy Cain. Instead, as the *Gazette* reported, "The lynching grew from threats that Joe made while under arrest as an accessory before the crime. He is charged with having said he only wanted a chance to kill Bud Harper." The identity or composition of the lynch mob was described with the label of "a posse of citizens."[21]

Act 258 would occasionally be referenced regretfully as an alternative to a lynching that had recently occurred. For example, on June 19, 1913, a Black man named Will Norman was lynched on a prominent downtown square in the spa resort of Hot Springs for allegedly having murdered the daughter of his employer. Following the lynching, Circuit Judge Calvin T. Cotham issued a statement in which he insisted, "A trial could have been had in 24 hours after the negro had been incarcerated in jail," adding, "It would have been a much better lesson had he been executed after a fair trial, not by self-appointed executioners who had neither legal nor moral right to take away his life."[22]

However, one has to ask—was there much difference, essentially, between a lynching and the successful execution of the law according to Act 258? Likely the most well-known implementation of Act 258 occurred in the wake of the Catcher Race Riot in the Arkansas River bottoms near the Oklahoma state line. On December 28, 1923, a white woman named Effie Latimer, aged twenty-five, was found by a neighbor mortally wounded in her house, having apparently been shot in the back with a shotgun, as well as beaten and cut all over her body. Before she died, she reportedly gave a description of her attacker, and on the basis of this description, authorities arrested a thirty-two-year-old Black man named William "Son" Bettis, who went peacefully along with the sheriff despite a claim of having been picking cotton when the crime occurred. The next day, police arrested two more Black men, the twenty-six-year-old Charles Spurgeon Ruck and fourteen-year-old John Henry Clay. As rumors spread, some two hundred men gathered on the courthouse lawn in Van Buren, the county seat, leading authorities to take their prisoners across the river to Fort Smith for safekeeping. Learning this, more than five hundred people congregated around the county jail in Fort Smith, forcing authorities to evacuate two of the men down to the state capital in Little Rock. Being unable to lynch these prisoners, the mob ran rampant through the primarily Black community of Catcher, murdering Ruck's father and reportedly burning down Black-owned homes and desecrating the cemetery. In response to a group of African American men barricading themselves, armed, in a log cabin for protection, authorities called out the National Guard, which arrived with a machine gun and secured the surrender and arrest of the men.

It was in this environment that the first trial, of Bettis and Ruck, began on January 4–5, 1924, but a week after the initial crime, in accordance with Act 258. Echoing the rhetoric employed by Father Lucey in his defense of the law, local newspapers made no pretentions about the possibility of innocence for the men, reporting on the event under the headline "Brutal Black Murderers on Trial for Most Inhuman Act." In the one-day trial of Ruck, the jury deliberated for just ten minutes before rendering a guilty verdict and sentencing him to die, and Bettis was similarly condemned the following day. Clay, who had testified against the other two men (and was, according to some accounts, subjected to torture to extract such testimony), was put on trial in March and sentenced to hard labor, though he later died in prison. Shortly after the trials of Ruck and Bettis, notices began circulating around Catcher demanding that all Black residents pack up and leave or face the consequences.[23]

Can one imagine a genuinely fair trial occurring in such circumstances? Of course not. The point, it would seem, is rather to have the "necessary" violence—such as the execution of Bettis and Ruck later that year—performed by representatives of the state acting in an official capacity rather than by the citizenry. This is the basis of the classical social contract, summarized thusly by philosopher Paul Dumouchel: "By renouncing our right to violence (and vengeance), we give the state the monopoly over violence. What we transfer is what we have 'renounced,' in other words, our violence. The unanimous transfer transforms the violence: *it makes it legitimate*. Thus, the state's coercive power no longer seems to be real violence, exactly, or rather, it becomes *good violence*, the purpose of which is peace, in opposition to *bad violence*, which creates disorder."[24]

So Act 258 could be seen as an attempt, no matter how ineffective, to transform illegitimate violence into legitimate, bad violence into good. It also transformed *subjective* violence into *objective* violence—or, perhaps more accurately, showed that lynching was but the subjective manifestation of already extant systems of objective violence. These terms, borrowed from the work of philosopher Slavoj Žižek, will require a modicum of explication. Subjective violence, simply put, has a subject. If I suddenly strike you, you can easily identify me as the perpetrator of violence and you as its victim, its subject. As Žižek writes, "Subjective violence is experienced as such against the background of a non-violent zero level. It is seen as a perturbation of the 'normal,' peaceful state of things." However, objective violence is "invisible since it sustains the very zero-level standard against which we perceive something as subjectively violent."[25] It is the good violence of peace, as Dumouchel put it.

Another way of differentiating these is to distinguish between the violence of killing, and the violence of "letting die." As geographer James Tyner writes, "The determination of violence, especially criminal violence, is neither neutral nor objective." He adds, "What if, for the moment, we consider violence to be any action or inaction that results in injury, maldevelopment, or death? In other words, what if we moved beyond an individually oriented and biologically premised understanding of violence to consider how certain policies, practices, and programs may have the same consequences for human survivability?"[26] This notion builds upon the foundational work of sociologist Johan Galtung, who defined violence as "present when human beings are being influenced so that their actual somatic and mental realizations are below their potential realizations." Violence, in other words, is "the cause of the difference between the potential and the actual."[27] Galtung described violence committed by an actor as personal or direct, while violence lacking an actor he termed structural or indirect, the latter being violence that "is built into the structure and shows up as unequal power and consequently unequal life chances."[28]

This may seem a bit abstract at present, so let us consider the following example. Popular culture, from novels like *Goldfinger* to the movie *Batman Begins*, is rife with the trope of some terrorist agent or evil mastermind poisoning a municipal water supply. We recognize this action as violence, and if some individual or organization did actually introduce poison into a local water source, our government would have no problem justifying the arrest, trial, and punishment of the perpetrators—even if they only attempted the deed but failed, they would still be found culpable of criminal misdeeds. But what if the water supply was contaminated not by shady terrorists but, instead, by a city council who voted to draw water from a source known or suspected to contain toxins? This happened most notably in Flint, Michigan, but hundreds and thousands of municipalities across the United States are subject to similar contamination, if not necessarily due to the deliberate acts of city councils, then due to aging and failing water infrastructure not being repaired or replaced, despite an awareness of the long-term effects of contaminated drinking water. These policies and practices have much the same result, in terms of injury, but are typically not regarded as violent due to (1) matters of intent, such as simply saving money versus hoping to kill or maim; (2) the distribution of responsibility from one individual or organization to allegedly democratically elected councils (and, by extension, to the entire population of voters); and (3) and the perceived moral difference between action and inaction. However, as philosopher Claudia Card writes, "Those who neglect or bring about others' poverty can be as morally reprehensible as terrorists."[29]

With Act 258, we see the state of Arkansas working to transform the subjective, personal violence of lynching into the objective or structural violence of the judicial system. Granted, the judicial and political system already functioned alongside vigilante violence as a mechanism of oppression for men and women, especially African Americans. As sociologist Mattias Smångs has observed, the removal of African Americans from political and social spheres during the so-called Jim Crow period did not diminish mob violence but, instead, increased it, as disfranchisement and lynching "complemented each other in promoting and enacting white group unity and power."[30] No accident, then, that the 1890s in Arkansas witnessed the culmination of efforts to deprive African Americans of the vote—first, with an election law in 1891 that consolidated control of the voting process in the hands of the state, ruled at this time by the Democratic Party, and then the following year with a constitutional amendment requiring payment of a poll tax to vote—as well as the greatest number of lynchings in the state for any decade.[31]

Political disfranchisement went hand in hand with economic marginalization, for without a political voice, those very same people who were most often targeted by lynch mobs could not hope to rein in the regimes of economic oppression inflicted upon them. As historian John William Graves has observed, following the Civil War on up through the early twentieth century, "poverty and inequality were widespread in the rural South," where "opportunities for economic and social mobility for plantation workers were greatly restricted and limited."[32]

The sharecropping system worked to keep Black laborers in perpetual debt to their employers, and education was often forbidden, or limited, for poor African Americans. For example, William Pickens, whose family migrated from South Carolina to Arkansas in the late 1880s, recalled that, during their first year in the state, the children of the family could not go to school but had to work the fields in order to pay off their immediate debt to the landlord; after the first year, however, his father "came home with sad, far-away eyes, having been told that we were deeper in debt than on the day of our arrival. And who could deny it? The white man did all the reckoning. The Negro did all the work."[33] At the same time that Black Arkansans were being disfranchised from the political sphere and oppressed in the economic, they were also increasingly subjected to segregated social spaces through laws such as the Separate Coach Law of 1891, which mandated separate railway cars for Black and white passengers, and the Streetcar Segregation Act of 1903, which assigned Black and white passengers segregated sections of city streetcars.[34] Too, as will be discussed in the final chapter, anti-miscegenation laws outlawed interracial cohabitation, thus segregating the most personal of spaces.

This, of course, does not even scratch the surface of the oppression faced by certain populations in Arkansas and beyond—all of it the result of policies, and all of these policies reinforcing each other, as segregation laws, for example, increased the social distance between Black and white Arkansans and thus decreased the potential for cross-racial solidarity. As anthropologist Akhil Gupta writes, "What makes this violence structural is that these unfortunate outcomes result from the *deliberate* actions of social agents. We have to keep in mind that certain classes of people have a stake in perpetuating a social order in which such extreme suffering is not only tolerated but also taken as normal."[35]

And one of the means for perpetuating that social order was lynching. White mobs regularly attacked educators and those who resisted being forced into the regime of plantation labor. In June 1897, for example, a mob attacked a Black school in Lonoke County in central Arkansas and beat the local teacher, D. T. Watson. As one national newspaper report recounted, mob leaders "told the negroes that they wanted them to chop cotton; that they had education enough." Watson soon went missing, his body later being discovered hanging from a tree and bearing the sign, "A warning to 'nigger' schoolteachers. We want none of this kind of people in this country; others beware."[36] Likewise, in June 1919, Clyde Ellison of Star City in southeastern Arkansas was lynched for reportedly refusing to work for a white farmer, Dave Bennett, for the sum of eighty-five cents a day. In response to this impertinence, Bennett had his daughter, Idelle, manufacture a charge of assault against Ellison, with hopes that this would scare him into working, but still he refused. Finally Ellison was seized, carried to a bridge, and hanged, with the mob later tacking to his body a sign reading, "This is how we treat lazy niggers."[37] In addition, white vigilantes drove many Black settlers away from their homesteads and many Black laborers away from emerging industries, such as mining and timber, during the late nineteenth and early twentieth centuries, given that whites often viewed industrial work as their own, especially since it paid better than a sharecropper's (often nonexistent) earnings.[38]

Objective violence made the subjective possible, but subjective violence can constitute a problem for modernizing states. And Arkansas was attempting to become more modern under Governor Donaghey, who had, in April 1909, signed into law Act 100, which created four regional agricultural schools that would, in the coming years, all become major universities. Donaghey would lead other major Progressive programs, such as the adoption of ballot initiatives and referenda, and the creation of a state board of health.[39] So it is no accident that he actively worked to prevent a lynching in early 1909 by sending the state guard to El Dorado, nor that he signed into law Act 258, because a modernizing state is a state that can brook no competitors for ultimate authority, for legitimacy— and lynching, ultimately, constitutes such a contention. As Dumouchel writes, "We can define as political all *violence that legitimizes itself*. Violence that is legitimate because the person who exercises it is a representative of the state's (legitimate) authority is either military or legal violence. Violence that fails to legitimize itself is criminal. Political violence is violence that becomes legitimate through the simple fact that it occurs."[40] Through its failure to prevent lynching and punish its perpetrators, the state made lynching legitimate violence—all the more so because such violence, especially in the late nineteenth and early twentieth centuries, became increasingly racialized, targeting African Americans almost exclusively and thus lining up with official state policies of white supremacy. Act 258 can, in this light, be regarded less as an actual attempt to reduce lynching but, rather, to strip the mob of its veneer of authority—to reiterate the state's claim to possess a monopoly on legitimate violence.

As noted, Governor Donaghey called out the state guard in 1909 to protect two men from being lynched in El Dorado. As it happens, the following year, on September 2,

1910, he called out troops again—but this time, to ensure that a Black teenager would be hanged. The young man in question, Harry Poe, allegedly raped (or attempted to assault) a white girl named Lena Adams in Hot Springs in early January 1910, and it was a wonder he was not lynched then. A posse, numbering about one hundred, went in search for Poe armed with Winchester rifles, and as the *Arkansas Gazette* reported, "there is an unspoken understanding among the citizens and should the fugitive be located, little doubt is expressed but that he will be shot by members of the posse."[41] However, Poe was arrested on January 26 and quickly taken to the state penitentiary at Little Rock.[42] During Poe's trial, Governor Donaghey ordered state troops to Hot Springs to prevent "any demonstration of violence," and Poe was quickly convicted on March 1 and sentenced to die a month later, though the Arkansas Supreme Court issued a stay of execution to allow for an appeal.[43] In May, the court upheld the death sentence.[44]

This is where the case takes an unexpected turn, with Poe's attorney filing a petition for a rehearing, based partly upon the support of a "delegation of society women from Hot Springs."[45] Two of these white women from Hot Springs even visited Governor Donaghey to petition him for clemency, insisting that Poe had been elsewhere at the time of the alleged attack upon Lena Adams. Donaghey refused to get involved in the matter, and the state Supreme Court denied the petition for a rehearing.[46] However, as the time drew near for the execution, local authorities began to worry that "sympathizers" might try to interfere with the hanging, and so the governor ordered a company of troops to the city of Hot Springs in order to ensure that the execution went through, in addition to turning down one last appeal for clemency.[47] Poe was executed at noon.

Such executions as that of Harry Poe—and even of the aforementioned Ruck and Bettis in 1924—are often called "legal lynchings." As criminal justice expert Margaret Vandiver has observed, those crimes typically referenced to justify lynching, such as murder and rape, that were the subject of Act 258, were the same ones that often earned a penalty of death, Too, as she states, "Often the same arguments were made to justify lynching and capital punishment, indicating that the practices may have served similar functions. Crime prevention was a primary justification for both forms of lethal punishment. . . . In addition both were considered necessary as a means of retribution for crimes the community would not tolerate."[48] In other words, these "legal lynchings" could be said to constitute the objective equivalent of subjective violence— the term does not make sense otherwise.

As we noted, subjective violence is political. But what about objective violence? Can objective violence be political? With an expansive view of the political, the question is practically tautological, given that objective violence arises from policies, and official policies are typically generated collectively—even if they are generated by one solitary person, an absolute dictator, they are nonetheless carried out by countless others whose obeisance lends those policies legitimacy. In other words, objective violence implicates more than just an easily defined perpetrator, bystander, or beneficiary of wrongdoing. The literary theorist Michael Rothberg has coined the term *implicated subject* to describe those who "occupy positions aligned with power and privilege without themselves being direct agents of harm; they contribute to, inhabit, inherit, or benefit from regimes of domination but do not originate or control such regimes. An implicated subject is neither a victim not a perpetrator, but rather a participant in histories and social formations that generate the positions of victim and perpetrator, and yet in which most people do not occupy such clear-cut roles."[49] Objective violence implicates more than perpetrators and bystanders—it implicates those who support, even if only monetarily (e.g., through taxes or purchases), the structure through which objective violence is made manifest. As Card has written, "An evil or an injustice is most apt to be explicitly called 'structural' when the responsible structure is not self-consciously created or administered, when there is not a conspicuous tyrant or tyrannical group, or when the practice comes over time to be interconnected with other practices in ways not specifically intended and then, owing to those connections, has consequences not specifically intended."[50]

Probably the most eloquent and evasive expression of the idea of the implicated subject, and the possibilities for structural violence, in Arkansas history was the conclusion of the Pulaski County grand jury investigation into the March 5, 1959, fire at the Negro Boys Industrial School, a juvenile work farm and reformatory for Black teenagers in Wrightsville. At the time the fire ignited for unknown reasons early that morning, the dormitory doors were locked from the outside, as was practice, and so the boys had to find their way through the smoke and flames to the windows and then bash through the screens to get outside. Forty-eight children survived; twenty-one died. State officials expressed horror at the deaths but had never once expressed interest in the lives confined therein, and those lives were rough. As Grif Stockley, historian of the fire, has written, "Though slavery was officially dead, the prison farm atmosphere eerily mimicked some of its most degrading and brutal features. In significant ways, the job of superintendent and staff roughly corresponded to that of plantation overseers and slave drivers."[51] The industrial education promised at the "school" consisted mostly of farm labor, runaways were whipped upon return, the boys often had only rags for clothes and lacked bedding and bathwater, and the buildings were regularly in grievous need of repair—which fact likely caused the fire. By the time its investigation wrapped up the following year, the Pulaski County grand jury wrote:

> The blame can be placed on lots of shoulders for the tragedy: the Board of Directors, to a certain extent, who might have pointed out through newspaper and other publicity the extreme hazards and plight of the school; the Superintendent and his staff, who perhaps continued to do the best they could in a resigned fashion when they had nothing to do with [it]; the State Administration, one right after another through the past years, who allowed conditions to become so disreputable; the General Assembly of the State of Arkansas, who should have been so ashamed of conditions that they would have previously allowed sufficient money to have these conditions corrected; and finally on the people of Arkansas, who did nothing about it.[52]

It is certainly possible to read such a conclusion in a cynical manner. After all, when everyone is responsible, no one is functionally responsible, even for a death toll that in other circumstances would have been labeled a massacre. But is this not the same approach taken by so many to lynching? After all, in promoting his bill, Father Lucey said that (white) men were "impelled to do this ugly work solely because there is no other means at hand of meting out proper justice." And Judge Grace, investigating that lynching in Pine Bluff, acknowledged, "The white man's blood boils when the honor of our women is attacked." Newspapers often went further, however, portraying lynching as not only necessary, in a regretful and unfortunate sense, but even natural. On December 31, 1904, the citizens of Newport in northeastern Arkansas lynched a white man named Louis Allwhite who, together with his son Newton, was accused of raping and murdering two women outside of town on Christmas Day. The *Arkansas Gazette* asserted, a few days after the lynching, that "the best and most effective deterrent from crime is competent and remorseless courts," but added that the confession Newton Allwhite had provided authorities was "enough to make the lynching spirit burn hot in the blood of even a law-abiding people."[53] Even more forcefully, following the 1913 lynching of the African American Will Norman in Hot Springs, the *Gazette* editorialized: "But everybody knows that there may come times when the anger of a community cannot be controlled and when the people cannot be restrained from wreaking vengeance on the meanest and lowest of mankind. Every community should pray that it may escape one of the awful crimes that have so often caused the forming of a lynching mob. But unfortunately such a crime cannot be guarded against any more than can the lightning stroke be held back in the heavens."[54]

As philosopher Mikkel Thorup has noted regarding such framing of violent deeds, "The other is *violence incarnate*, while I am only *violent incidental*. This leads to the utmost important conclusion: the violence of the other perpetuates and perhaps even universalizes violence, whereas my violence promises an end to violence."[55] Even the blood of a law-abiding people might burn hot, and their vengeance cannot be constrained. Just as the grand jury report implicated the entire population of Arkansas for the conditions at the Arkansas Negro Boys Industrial School that produced the fire that killed twenty-one young men, so, too, did the newspapers of an earlier era implicate all humanity in the public butchery of lynching. To flip the script—if no one was responsible, then everyone was responsible. The anger of a community cannot be controlled.

Of course, it was not anger that resulted in the deaths of those twenty-one boys at Wrightsville—it was policy. Unlike lynching, there need not have been any specific racial animus in the development of the various policies that produced the deaths of those boys. As legal expert Michelle Alexander has written, the way we understand typical racism (and violence) has been "shaped by the most extreme expressions of individual bigotry, not by the way in which it functions naturally, almost invisibly (and sometimes with genuinely benign intent), when it is embedded in the structure of a social system."[56] Such "structural racism" has been the subject of a growing body of scholarship and can be defined, according to sociologist Tanya Maria Golash-Boza, as "inter-institutional interactions across time and space that reproduce racial inequality."[57] Because of the structural, institutional nature of racism and its attendant violence, we have a real difficulty in recognizing those deaths in Wrightsville as anything other than "tragic." As Tyner writes, "Our a priori abstractions of violence mask certain actions—and most inactions—as violent. In turn, our ability to see (certain) actions and inactions will affect our ensuring constitution of criminal behavior."[58] We can see the actions of lynching as criminal behavior, but it is more difficult for us to recognize exactly how lynching arose from larger-scale actions and inactions, what Žižek describes as "the more subtle forms of coercion that sustain relations of domination and exploitation, including the threat of violence."[59] This is because lynching was also policy, even if the state did occasionally make noise about the distastefulness of vigilante violence. After all, it was policy that kept African Americans an impoverished and immobile workforce, and the lynching of people like Clyde Ellison, for refusing to work for a poor wage, helped to reinforce that policy by making an example of him. Every lynching was a message, a warning to stay in line with the policies that made life unbearable. In other words: "This is how we treat lazy niggers."

Let us go back, in closing, to Act 258. As Tyner has written, "What we may understand (and potentially criminalize) as violence is itself the outcome of political practice—practice that is conditioned by any given social formation. The constitution of violence, in other words, is internal to the social relations of any given society."[60] But Act 258 did not understand or even potentially criminalize lynching as violence—the social relations in the state of Arkansas at the time militated against such a conclusion. Even the author of the bill, Father Lucey, seemed to regard lynching as something distasteful, like the processing of meat, that was probably best left to the experts, to the system, there being no need for "men of high character to imbrue their hands in the blood of a negro brute."

Recall Dumouchel's view of political violence as that which legitimates itself. He expounds upon this idea further:

> Political violence is violence in which people other than those who originally commit it see themselves and are ready to participate. The political dimension of violence does not depend

on any specific feature of the action, but is based on the transfer to those who commit the violent action of the violence of (some among) those who do not commit it. If this transfer does not occur, the violence is only a crime that requires redress. *All political violence is an exercise in shifting the violence of some onto acceptable targets, sacrificable victims.*[61]

Those who did not participate in the actual act of lynching readily identified with it. As we have seen, and will see again in numerous examples, the ostensible best and brightest of society regularly embraced lynching as a necessary measure for punishing those (especially Black men) who committed "infamous" crimes. Even when people like Father Lucey opposed the form of lynching, they nonetheless publicly expressed sympathies with the people who found themselves sufficiently aroused by circumstance to commit such atrocities. And by so doing, such ostensible opponents of lynching lent the practice legitimacy: "The more people identify with the violence," writes Dumouchel, "the greater its political worth will be, and the more it becomes legitimate."[62] Father Lucey may have thought that by trying to meet the mob halfway with expressions of understanding, he could convince them to lay aside their butchery, but by so doing, he ceded the entire argument to the lynchers. Moreover, he ensured that his precious law would be nothing more than lynching by another name.

3

HUMANISM

... as in Arkansas once, a man proved guilty by law,
of murder, but whose condemnation was deemed
unjust by the people, so that they rescued him to try
him themselves; whereupon, they, as it turned out,
found him even guiltier than the court had done,
and forthwith proceeded to execution; so that the
gallows presented the truly warning spectacle of a
man hanged by his friends.

—Herman Melville, *The Confidence-Man*

WERE WE TO ATTEMPT to rank the various lynchings in Arkansas by the rather subjective category of the brutality on display—acknowledging that each lynching was a uniquely brutal display of violence its own right, irrespective of the identity of the person butchered or his supposed crime—we would likely have to put the 1921 killing of Henry Lowery near the top.

Lowery was a laborer on the plantation of O. T. Craig, a seventy-year-old landowner in Mississippi County in the northeastern corner of Arkansas. This was cotton country; the flat Delta land was made rich by the river that gave the county its name, while the people who owned the land were made rich by systems of exploitation such as sharecropping and debt peonage. Lowery was one of those exploited people, having worked about two years for Craig before that fatal Christmas Day of 1920. That was the day Lowery went to the Craig house to demand a cash settlement for his work. As historian Karlos Hill writes, "Within the plantation economy, asking for a payment settlement was considered a subversive act that directly threatened the façade of debt upon which sharecropping was premised."[1] White newspapers liked to report that Lowery was drunk when he arrived at the Craig plantation house, in keeping with well-worn tropes of the "worthless negro," but a man like Lowery might well need a stiff drink before taking such a radical step as to demand payment rather than submit to the endless drudgery, the bare life he was afforded by the system. And this, according to some reports, was not the first time Lowery had dared to press for a settlement.

When he showed up at the Craig house on Christmas Day, Craig apparently attacked him. Lowery retreated, only to have Craig's son Richard shoot him as he fled. In response, Lowery returned fire, and his aim was better—he wounded two of Craig's sons, and killed Craig's daughter and Craig himself.

Ten years before this, another Black sharecropper, Steve Green, in neighboring Crittenden County, had fled to Chicago after killing his employer, William Malcolm Sidle, in self-defense, and after his arrest barely escaped extradition to Arkansas.[2] Lowery went in the opposite direction, down to El Paso, Texas, but a letter back to his family in Arkansas was intercepted and led authorities to his location on January 19, 1921. Upon his arrest, Lowery reportedly begged his captors to kill him or provide him a razor to do it himself, knowing the fate that awaited him. "The fact that Lowery preferred suicide," writes

Hill, "is not surprising, particularly given the brutality he likely imagined would be exacted upon his body during a lynching."³ Police, however, are not typically given to accommodating such requests, although Governor Thomas McRae of Arkansas did agree to hold Lowery at the state penitentiary in Little Rock for safekeeping to prevent an outbreak of mob violence.

The deputies from Arkansas did not concern themselves with the governor's orders to transport their prisoner directly from El Paso to Little Rock. Instead, they took a circuitous route through New Orleans and then Sardis, Mississippi; as Hill writes, the route taken by these deputies "suggests that Arkansas authorities more than likely colluded with mob leaders, establishing the Sardis train station as the prearranged rendezvous point for handing over Lowery to them. In fact, approximately thirty minutes before the train carrying Lowery arrived at the Sardis station, a mob of fifteen to twenty men was waiting for its arrival in a hotel lobby."⁴ The mob took possession of Lowery without any resistance from his appointed guardians and proceeded to return to the scene of the crime, although not before purchasing rope and having lunch in Millington, Tennessee, all without the slightest interference from the police in any of the three states they traversed that fateful day.

The *care* with which Lowery was slowly and painfully murdered on January 26, 1921, reveals some important, and often unrecognized, characteristics of the practice of lynching. First, there was the care devoted to Lowery's comfort before the lynching. As the *Arkansas Gazette* and other newspapers reported, Lowery was allowed to make requests of his captors: "The negro was asked if there was anything he wanted before punishment was inflicted. He said he would like to have food. This was given him. Then he asked to be permitted to say good-by to his wife and children, and they were summoned. However, they left before the torch was applied."[5] As will be discussed in chapter 5, this is the sort of care we can expect to accord with mimetic theory. As the theologian Wolfgang Palaver writes, "The executed victims, perceived by the community as guilty criminals, represent in obvious fashion the initial negative transference. We see elements of the positive transference, too, however, in the veneration shown even to criminals awaiting execution. Very weakened forms of this veneration can be observed even in our contemporary age. One considers the French custom in which the prisoner sentenced to death was permitted a cigarette and a glass of rum, or the ritual of the 'last meal' for death-row inmates on the day of their execution."[6]

Then there was the care devoted to ensuring his agony as the process of lynching went under way. The same *Gazette* report emphasizes that the mob "went about the lynching in a quiet and orderly manner," choosing "a spot well concealed from the public road by a heavy clump of bushes, just across the levee from Nodena and within sight of the Craig plantation home." There, the report went, "the negro was chained to a log. A pile of brush was placed around him and a match applied." But this particular death by burning was intended to be as painful as possible. As Hill writes, "Reports emphasized that Lowery's body burned for thirty or forty minutes before he died. Apparently, as Lowery's body was burning, he attempted to inhale smoke from the fire to hasten his death, but a mob participant intervened to prevent this."[7]

Why the torture? This was not torture as practiced in the classical and medieval worlds: to elicit a confession or to save someone's soul ultimately from the fires of hell. Regarding the Spanish Inquisition, that archetypal agency of atrocity, historian Henry Kamen writes, "Torture was employed exclusively to elicit information or a confession, and never used as a punishment."[8] But this was torture precisely as punishment, although not corrective punishment, since the torturers in question had no intention of letting Lowery survive his agony, and neither did they care for his immortal soul. No doubt the torture was intended as a warning to others about the dangers of defiance. As the philosopher Claudia Card has observed, "Torture was widely used in the twentieth century in Chile, Argentina, and elsewhere to intimidate others who were not in custody."[9] As we discussed regarding the production of terror in chapter 1, the slow roasting of Lowery would serve a similar purpose—namely, to stem a possible tide of resistance to planter rule in the Delta. Perhaps the memory of Steve Green still circulated among planters, and so, when confronted with the opportunity to make Lowery pay with his life, they made the most of it.

Such violence is typically regarded as the result of a long campaign and culture of dehumanization, resulting in a fundamental lack of empathy for the person or persons targeted for torture, murder, expulsion, or other evils. Human rights scholar Kjell Anderson has noted that "when perpetrators receive relentless messages from trusted sources dehumanizing the victim group, it is likely that this will alter or erode their previously held views."[10] "Violence is prepared through rhetorical excess," writes philosopher Mikkel Thorup. "The language of violence prepares and enables the practice of violence."[11] Part of that rhetorical excess is a powerful binary of purity versus impurity, as applied to entire populations, so common to oppressive and even genocidal regimes. As historian Eric D. Wietz notes, "Those who were considered unclean were an active source of pollution that threatened to contaminate the clean and the pure. Hence they had to be at least quarantined and, in the most extreme cases, eradicated altogether."[12] In the American South, this binary broke down along racial and gender lines that warped social interaction between racial groups in such a way as to justify lynching for a range of behaviors due to the fundamental threat of pollution that was offered; or as historian Jacqueline Dowd Hall writes, "The 'false chivalry' of lynching cast [white] women as Christ-like symbols of racial purity and regional identity and translated every sign of Black self-assertion into a metaphor for rape—black over white, a world turned upside down."[13]

In Arkansas during the period when lynching was most common, newspapers remained the most trusted and widespread sources of information available to the general public, and as historian Randy Finley has found, the words that the most popular state newspaper of the time applied to African American lynching victims explicitly removed them from the realm of humanity: "The terms of choice used by the *Arkansas Gazette* to describe those lynched for sexual crimes were *ravager, fiend,* and *brute.* . . . By calling those accused and lynched 'brutes,' the 'responsible' citizens of a community, now murderers, rationalized their behavior."[14] Not only that—according to Fritz Breithaupt, such propaganda can help to diminish any empathy one might feel toward a person's suffering by interpreting it as just: "Most of us feel less empathetic when we think someone deserves punishment. The attribution of guilt, therefore, could serve as a catalyst for the blocking of empathy."[15] Or as the philosopher Kate Manne notes, the altruism we often assume to lie at the core of humanity is perpetually "mediated by political ideologies, hierarchies, and the associated sense of entitlement—and hence subsequent needs and aggression when those needs are thwarted."[16] This means that, when it comes to matters of "us" and "them," our self-identification may not be with "human beings *writ large*; it may be human beings in a *particular social position* or who occupy a certain *rank* in one of many potential intra-human hierarchies (including those that have their basis in supposed moral values)."[17]

Even when discussing Black Arkansans not accused of horrible misdeeds, dehumanization was at play in the media of the day, as African Americans were typically depicted as lazy, filthy, ignorant—all without a thought on the part of writers as to why they might manifest these apparent traits. As Anderson has written, "Dehumanization is often a self-fulfilling prophecy, as perpetrators consign their victims to situations in which they will manifest the desired characteristics."[18] In other words, African Americans were dehumanized by means of the structural violence, outlined in the previous chapter, that constituted life in Arkansas for so many. And this gets to the core of the issue, for oppression need not necessarily arise as the consequence of dehumanization but, rather, can be the means of perfecting that process, of rendering an individual or an entire population as less than human. According to the philosopher David Livingstone Smith, "The desire to harm others leads to their dehumanization, rather than the other way around. It liberates antagonisms that are already there, simmering in the background and just waiting to burst out, or ratchets up the violence already being done."[19] As philosopher Berel Lang writes, "The process of systematic dehumanization requires a conscious affirmation of the wrong involved in it—that is, that someone who is human should be made to seem, to become, and in any event to be treated as less than that."[20] Such a process constitutes one of the under-appreciated facets of the Holocaust, to give one example:

> But neither during that time nor subsequently was there any doubt about the systematic brutality and degradation which figured in Nazi policy and which itself, by a cruel inversion, testified more strongly even than extermination itself to the essentially human status accorded the Jews to begin with. In the face of alleged danger, a justification for violence based on the right of self-defense can plausibly be invoked. But a systematic pattern of torture and degradation is only intelligible on the premise that the victims are not essentially dissimilar from the perpetrators and that something much more morally complex than self-defense is at issue.[21]

A very popular quotation, attributed to US Army psychologist Captain G. M. Gilbert, who was assigned to observe defendants at the Nuremburg trials, insists that evil is the absence of empathy, "a genuine incapacity to feel with their fellow men." This statement holds with the general thesis that perpetrators of atrocity had dehumanized those against whom they directed violence. But what if the lynching of Lowery, and other cases of racial violence, stemmed not so much from dehumanization but, rather, a recognition of the humanity of the victim—and a desire to destroy that humanity? What if empathy was not the missing ingredient in these social relationships but, instead, the most dangerous?

The exact connection between evil and empathy has

been questioned in recent years by scholars, among them the aforementioned Breithaupt, who writes, "Sometimes we commit atrocities not out of a failure of empathy but rather as a direct consequence of successful, even overly successful, empathy."[22] This may sound absurd, but one should note that most conflicts that arise are not limited to an individual self and an individual other but rather have a group component, either a group against an individual or groups against each other, and so there are multiple parties to consider. As Breithaupt writes, "Among the most significant catalyst for empathizing is the dynamic of *side-taking*: when the observer is witness to two parties in conflict and decides to support one."[23] In an environment in which racial differences had been heavily naturalized through propaganda of all sorts, it is perhaps not surprising that people who had no connection at all to the events that drove the lynching of Henry Lowery—or any lynching at all—would be so quick to take sides. Many white elites of the day, knowing themselves precariously positioned atop a pyramid of white supremacy that could not help but drive resentment, would immediately identify with the slain planter, as he was one of them, while middle- and lower-class whites, who had long been trained to see association with their economic and social betters as the tickets to their own success, or at least saw those people as models to be emulated, would be more inclined to identify with elites with whom they at least shared a racial heritage. Empathy could drive them to be a part of the mob. "And while the side-taker," writes Breithaupt, "may not fully understand the side they are taking, share the feelings of the person whose position they have selected or perceive their intentions, the decision, we assume, is based on their recognition of a *tendency* in their chosen side that is derived from perceivable actions and inclinations."[24]

Far from ameliorating conflicts, empathy can actually serve to exacerbate them; terrorists, for example, "can act out of empathy for those in whose name they kill; ethnic, religious, and political conflicts can arise and escalate because of empathy for the victims of oppression or injustice, whether real or imagined."[25] Remember that mainstream propaganda regularly depicted African Americans not simply as brutes and fiends but also, in their less violent manifestations, as lazy, shifty, devious— as people who are constantly looking to shirk their duties, probably so that they can go get drunk somewhere. Everyday life in a capitalist society was already an ongoing conflict against the nature of Black people.

Moreover, an expansive sense of empathy may well fuel the sort of sadism on evidence in the lynching of Lowery. According to Breithaupt:

> Punishing others provides an emotional reward. Anger and the chance to quench it through retribution seem to offer the necessary drive to punish. In this sense, the punisher is not acting altruistically [in the sense of doing something for the community at personal risk] but rather out of self-interest. Sadistic empathy, the pleasure of the pain of others who are punished, could have emerged in an evolutionary context as an impetus for punishing antisocial acts because it serves a function for the species as a whole. Seen this way, sadistic empathy makes sense, as it would have a selection advantage for the community.[26]

Such sadistic empathy in the form of punishment often exhibits a theatrical component, as we can see with the various "spectacle" lynchings that take place before massive crowds on the courthouse square. "Once a mass mob had captured its victim, the selection of the site of execution, the act of execution, and the immediate aftermath of the lynching unfolded in a highly ritualized choreography," writes historian W. Fitzhugh Brundage.[27] The choice of site, in particular, was of great symbolic value, with many such mobs, as occurred in the case of Henry Lowery, choosing a site close to the original crime. "The scene of punishment," writes Breithaupt, "evokes and repeats the scene of the original wrongdoing. It perpetuates the presence of the past, and its ritualization allows the original act of violation to be repeated, like a film. Empathy with the victim of the prior violation," in this case O. T. Craig, "scripts how the subsequent punishment is observed."[28]

Our tendency to see acts like lynching as an aberration to normal human concourse finds reflection in how we view hatred as the antithesis of more sociable emotions like love (never mind that shared hatred can often serve as the basis of social cohesion). However, as psychologists Robert J. and Karin Sternberg declare rather bluntly, "hate is very closely related psychologically to love."[29] In fact, the Sternbergs identify three components to love—intimacy, passion, and commitment—two of which are present in hate, with the third, intimacy, being replaced by its negation. This forms what they call the triangular theory of the structure of hate. Love and hate both entail passion, or "sources of motivational and other forms of arousal," as well as commitment, or a determination to maintain a relationship, but where love requires intimacy, a feeling of closeness and connectedness, hate entails the opposite, an "emotional distance" from an individual who "arouses repulsion and disgust."[30] As the Sternbergs write:

Negation of intimacy may arise when there were no particular feelings beforehand. An individual may come to be hated because he or she has, or is perceived to have, committed a crime against one's person. In the case of a sexual crime, a reaction of disgust and revulsion is common. Negation of intimacy comes to be felt toward someone who previously had been unknown in one's life. The crime may be real or imagined. And the feelings may result not just in the victim of the crime, but in third parties who hear of the (alleged) crime and feel disgust or revulsion toward the (alleged) perpetrator.[31]

This can explain why white Southern paternalism, in which white elites regarded themselves as the beneficent protectors of Black Southerners, especially those whom they knew personally and regarded as the better exemplars "of their race," could so easily and quickly produce vigilante violence against the same population—and sometimes against the same people who were previously (comparatively) well regarded. The triadic relationship did not need to be built from scratch; all it took was the replacement of intimacy with its negation through allegations of criminal misdeed to transform the gentle Southern paternalist into the screeching mob leader. Far from representing the pinnacle of a process of dehumanization, the violent deeds of a mob or an individual can, in Manne's words, "often betray the fact that their victims must seem human, all too human, to perpetrators."[32]

Indeed, sometimes lynch mobs went out of their way to portray their actions as respectful of the humanity of their victims and, because of that, thus insisted upon the humanity of the mob's members. Such was the case with the August 9, 1916, lynching of an "unidentified negro," whose age was given as about twenty or twenty-five, in the southeastern Arkansas town of Stuttgart. On the afternoon of August 7, the unknown man, who was described as having "been loafing about Stuttgart for several days," reportedly perpetrated "an attack on the 16-year-old daughter of Ernest Wittman, a farmer near Stuttgart." He approached her while she "was in the field near her home," and "after asking several questions, attacked her." Wittman was able to break free and make her way home, but by the time she returned to the site of the attack with her mother, the assailant had fled.

As word spread in town, a posse formed, and the man was captured a few miles off and jailed in Stuttgart. With the threat of mob violence high, "the black was spirited away by the officers, who set out in the direction of Little Rock," leading to the belief that he had been taken to the state penitentiary, where many whose presence was likely to incite a lynching were temporarily housed through the years. However, the officers in question only took him so far as DeWitt, the county seat. The Wittman daughter was taken there to identify him, and she confirmed that the man was the perpetrator. This news, apparently, "caused the forming of the mob and the lynching of the negro," as "about 20 men in six automobiles" left Stuttgart for DeWitt, where they overpowered the jailer, secured his keys, and kidnapped the alleged attacker. About 1:00 a.m., the mob returned to Stuttgart, where "the black was taken to the negro section of the city and hanged to a tree in the center of the section. His body was riddled with bullets and the body was left hanging until 9 o'clock this morning, when it was cut down by local officers."[33]

Here, we can find tropes that have already appeared in

accounts of lynching elsewhere. Most notably, as detailed in chapter 1, this lynching serves as an act of terror. The accounts of the murder in the *Arkansas Democrat* and the *Pine Bluff Daily Graphic* specifically state that the man was unknown and that he had said to people that he came from Osceola in northeastern Arkansas. Despite this lack of any affiliation with the local Black population, he was nevertheless hanged by the mob in "the negro section of the city" of Stuttgart, thus reflecting what Arne Johan Vetlesen called the "logic of generic attribution." (In fact, as noted in chapter 1, about two months later another African American man would be taken from the jail at De Witt and lynched in the "negro section" of that particular town for allegedly having insulted two white women.[34]) Too, this line from the *Democrat* stands out: "He made no efforts to get work, and local officers believed that he was a tramp." So again, we have further, indirect justification of the lynching by having this particular victim conform to the "lazy negro" stereotype.

However, the most noteworthy aspect of this event is the later appeal to humanism on the part of the mob. Shortly after the lynching, a letter attributed only to "The Committee" was mailed to the *Stuttgart Free Press* and published on August 11 before being reprinted in the statewide *Arkansas Democrat*, under the title "Mob Victim Was Extended Every Earned Courtesy," a few days later. The letter reads as follows:

> We, members of the committee that hanged the negro Wednesday morning, have, after listening to the false stories about the affair, concluded that it is due to the public that they be made acquainted with the true facts.
>
> The criminal was taken from the jail at

DeWitt, brought to the scene of execution and hanged in as humane a manner as possible.

Quite recently, in England, a man was hanged for high treason. He suffered the tortures of strangulation for nine minutes before he was pronounced dead by the attending physicians. We give you our word that the criminal we "lynched" did not live nine seconds after his feet left the ground, as the shot wounds on his body will prove.

The only request made by the criminal was that he be hanged or shot and not tortured or burned. That his request was granted was self-evident to every one who saw the remains.

We want also to say that the criminal made a full, free and voluntary confession of his guilt before being executed.

For obvious reasons, we must withhold our names, and beg to sign ourselves,

Yours for the proper and unfailing enforcement of the law.

THE COMMITTEE.[35]

The missive is interesting in how it frames the lynching in the most humanitarian way possible, especially through a comparison to recent proceedings of justice in that eminently more civilized nation of England. The committee is at pains to stress that their victim did not suffer in death and that he admitted to his crimes of his own free will. In addition, they refer to their actions as constituting an execution and even later put the word *lynch* in quotation marks.

All of this helps to chip away at what Manne calls the "'humanist' explanation for interpersonal conduct of the kind that is naturally described as *inhumane*," in which "such behavior often stems from people's failure to recognize some of their fellows *as* fellow human beings."[36] As she notes, there are significant problems with this particular framework for interpreting interpersonal violence and oppression:

> The humanist sense that something *is* needed by way of a special psychological story here is ... premised on the idea that it will typically be difficult for an agent to commit acts of violence or otherwise aggress against vulnerable and innocent parties. So something has to be done to alter the agent's perception of his soon-to-be victim. But this misses the fact that agents in a dominant social position often don't start out with such a neutral or salutary view of things. They are perpetually mired in certain kinds of *delusions* about their own social positions relative to other people, and their respective obligations, permissions, and entitlements. So, from the perspective of the dominant, the people they mistreat are often far from innocent. On the contrary, they are often tacitly—and falsely— held to be deeply guilty.[37]

If we return to the case of Henry Lowery, we can see many of these delusions at work. Craig believed that he was entitled to withhold from Lowery any cash settlement for his work and that Lowery was obligated to continue working for him, without protest, despite never receiving payment. But these were delusions shared by all the planter elite—and, by extension, all of white society. Another delusion was that a man had no right to self-defense if he were Black and his attacker white, and any act of self-preservation by a Black man could and should result in his lynching. These people knew that Lowery was human, and their sense of his humanity was manifest in their treatment of him before his murder. They brought him food and drink and allowed him to visit his wife and children. However, their conception of his humanity was heavily imbricated with a belief either in the innate sinfulness of African Americans or the necessity of keeping a Black workforce exploited and exploitable, or both, and so their sense of his humanity also manifested itself in the fire that consumed his body.

These delusions seem to be the source of the many inconsistencies in reports on lynching, especially when it comes to the motivation behind the violence. Consider the case of Clinton Briggs, lynched near Star City in southeastern Arkansas on September 1, 1919. According to state and local papers, Briggs, a veteran of World War I, was working on the plantation of J. M. Bailey when he encountered his employer's daughter, Ollie Bailey, "as she was driving some cows to pasture on her father's place." He reportedly then "stopped her and made an indecent proposal to her," upon which she "ran screaming to the house and acquainted the members of her family with the negroe's [sic] actions." The report admits a lack of detail regarding the subsequent events, save that Briggs "was held captive all day Monday by a party of about 30 men, and was shot while being taken to a tree to be hanged."[38] By contrast, a report on the lynching from the Chicago newspaper *The Whip* presents a different sequence of events:

> According to reports, Briggs was walking along the sidewalk, when he met a white couple, and as he stepped to one side to let them pass, the white

woman brushed into him and said, "Niggers get off of the sidewalk down here." Briggs replied that this was a free country. No sooner than he had made the remarks, the woman's escort seized him. As he tussled to get away from his opponent, other whites going along the street quickly ganged around. Briggs was quickly thrust into a passing automobile and was taken about two or three miles out from town, followed by three or four car loads of white hoodlums.

After the hoodlums had reached the edge of town, they found they could not secure a rope to lynch the innocent soldier with, so they took automobile chains and chained him to a tree, after which he was made the target of forty or fifty rifle and revolver bullets.[39]

Let us assume that the latter account is objectively true. In line with Manne's insight, the former account, which has Briggs making an indecent proposal to a woman, could be subjectively true for those living under the shared delusion of white supremacy and inherent Black inferiority and criminality. Nothing could be more indecent for a Black man, especially one recently returned from the war, than to assert that this is a free country. Such a statement easily could have provoked her companion into responding with force, and once the affair turned into a physical altercation between a Black man and a white man, the white men in the vicinity who witnessed the struggle knew instantly whom to blame without needing to know who actually threw the first punch.

The specific historical context in this case made an instant determination/delusion of guilt—and thus a lynching—all the more likely, for Black soldiers had returned from the European front with certain expectations for the full recognition of their citizenship. As historian David F. Krugler writes, "For African Americans, Wilson's call to war offered an opportunity to redress America's deficiencies. For doing their part to make the world safe for democracy, blacks expected restoration of voting rights in the South, an end to lynching and mob violence, and the dismantling of racial segregation."[40] White planter elites, leery of both empowering African Americans by giving them the chance to serve the military (where they would receive weapons training and have opportunities to use it against white Germans) and sending off to war the people who comprised their exploitable workforce, exerted influence on local draft boards to keep Black laborers where they were. As historian Nan Elizabeth Woodruff writes, "Arkansas in 1917 had to send 40 percent of its [draft-eligible] white population in order to meet its draft quota. Delta counties did not have enough white men to send, meaning that other portions of the state had to contribute much more than 40 percent to achieve the overall goal."[41] Too, during the war, whites were prone to imagining that African Americans might, in fact, be plotting against their rule through alliances with America's stated enemies. As historian Randy Finley writes, "War hysteria peaked in Calhoun County in April 1917 when blacks were arrested in wholesale quantity and ordered to cease holding meetings, whites fearing that Mexican agents had been contacted by Germans and were infiltrating Black organizations with seditious thought."[42] And almost as bad, if not worse, when Black men returned to their homes after their period of service, they expected the world to be different. In the face of these expectations, white planters moved to assert their dominance using three fundamental strategies identified by Woodruff:

> One involved the sharecropping system itself, which became even more oppressive and damaging to families. A second line of controls involved law and government, both used traditionally by white people in the American Congo to deny black people their rights and restrict their mobility— through controlling the mail system, overseeing contractual arrangements, enforcing convict labor, and denying them justice in the courts. Finally, they cemented this rule with outright terrorism, through lynching, daily violence, and the resurgence of the Ku Klux Klan. Remarkably, these measures failed to quash black resistance.[43]

Thus, in the postwar hotbed of paranoia in which whites were attempting, with greater and greater effort and desperation, to reassert their dominance, a Black man daring to describe the United States as a "free country" could be taken as a challenge to authority that must be resisted at all costs.

Look carefully at what is happening in this historical context, for it fundamentally challenges the idea that perpetrators of racial violence fundamentally fail to regard their targets as fully human. After all, white actions are a direct result of them being able to imagine African Americans as having their own wills and desires. They know that many Black men would welcome the opportunity to escape oppressive labor systems and undertake a service that better accords with their ideas of manhood. Whites can even foresee how such men will undergo an individual and collective change in their attitudes vis-à-vis whites upon their return home and will likely make further demands for economic independence and the right of political participation. Thus, in response to this, whites prepared themselves to employ violence where needed in order to maintain their relative privilege. Their willingness to engage in violence was predicated upon a realistic understanding of Black humanity, upon their ability to imagine how African Americans might act in these circumstances.

Philosophers use the term *theory of mind* for how human beings, on the basis of sensory input from one another, infer mental states in other humans. In fact, human beings having a theory of mind is what makes societies work, for without the ability to attribute desires, emotions, knowledge sets, and more to other people, combined with the ability to understand the myriad ways in which those mental states may differ from one's own, we would lack the necessary feedback loop to keep social concourse proceeding (and terror, as we saw in chapter 1, is a disruption of this feedback loop). During interpersonal interactions, we typically adopt what philosopher Daniel C. Dennett calls an intentional stance, in which we treat the other "as an agent, indeed a rational agent, who harbors beliefs and desires and other mental states that exhibit *intentionality* or 'aboutness,' and whose actions can be explained (or predicted) on the basis of the content of those states."[44] But theory of mind goes beyond Dennett's intentional stance. As psychologists Andrew Whiten and Josef Perner explain, "To arrive at what another individual sees or believes, one puts oneself mentally in his position ('putting oneself in another person's shoes') and estimates what one would see or believe oneself in that situation."[45]

A theory of mind is, essentially, based upon one's own self-awareness as a conscious being and an assumption that others have a similar experience of subjective selfhood, that they "have similar mental states in similar conditions," although "such differences between individuals as those of age and sex, political or religious belief, for example, are likely to make that assumption flawed."[46]

Whites not only possessed a theory of mind when it came to African Americans—they knew that African Americans possessed a theory of mind regarding whites. And this made the humanity of Black people all the more horrifying to whites. As Manne eloquently explicates:

> For a fellow human being is not just an intelligible *spouse, parent, child, sibling, friend, colleague,* etc. in relation to you and yours. They are also an intelligible *rival, enemy, usurper, insubordinate, betrayer,* etc. Moreover, in being capable of rationality, agency, autonomy, and judgment, they are also someone who could coerce, manipulate, humiliate, or shame you. In being capable of abstract relational thought and congruent moral emotions, they are capable of thinking ill of you and regarding you contemptuously. In being capable of forming complex desires and intentions, they are capable of harboring malice and plotting against you. In being capable of valuing, they may value what you abhor and abhor what you value. They may hence be a threat to all you cherish. And you may be a threat to all *they* cherish in turn—as you may realize. This provides all the more reason to worry about others' capacity for cruelty, contempt, malice, and so forth.[47]

This dynamic underscores the nature of white supremacist violence from the earliest days of slavery onward. After all, whites may have espoused rhetoric about slavery being the natural, preferred state for "negro brutes," but their actions demonstrated how much better they understood those whom they held in bondage, for they were perpetually on guard for the slightest signs of disobedience and revolt. As historian Kelly Houston Jones has demonstrated, even in Arkansas, a state that witnessed no actual slave revolts, whites stayed informed about such uprisings elsewhere in the United States and remained vigilant about the possibility of subaltern violence at home.[48]

Moreover, despite the supposed metaphysical difference between the two races, whites were often forced to acknowledge themselves as competitors with Black workers. According to historian Michael Pierce, the Mechanics Institute of Little Rock, one of the state's first labor unions, organized in 1858 in large part "to rid the city of all types of unfree and degraded labor, including not only slaves who competed with whites but also convicts and free blacks."[49] Among the political proposals supported by the Mechanics was the bill that eventually became Act 151 of 1859, which mandated the expulsion of free Blacks from the state; enslavers also supported this law out of fear that free Blacks proved a bad model for their own human property.[50] In post-emancipation Arkansas, whites continued to regard African Americans as rivals for limited resources, especially land and labor, and undertook campaigns of violence against them in ways that mirrored the antebellum dynamic—in part because they wanted such work themselves, and in part because Black laborers at work in industry, or Black homesteaders living independently upon their own land, could prove a bad model to others of their kind, who might desire such opportunities themselves.

The record is extensive on this front. In early 1883, white vigilantes attempted to drive off a Black man, Burrell Lindsay, from his legal homestead in Van Buren County in north central Arkansas. In January 1894, whitecappers in the northeastern town of Black Rock posted notices around town and specifically delivered written and verbal warnings to major employers, demanding that all businesses discharge their Black workers or have their property burned. (Employers could get away with paying Black workers less, which made their labor more attractive in many industries, as well as agriculture.) In Polk County along the western edge of the state in August 1896, white railroad workers (some of them European immigrants) teamed up with local white residents to drive away Black laborers brought in to work on what later became the Kansas City Southern Railroad; later that year, a number of sawmills across southern Arkansas witnessed deadly violence against African Americans. Three years later in the northeastern Arkansas town of Paragould, whitecappers posted notices and stoned residences and businesses in apparent protest of the importation of Black workers; a few years later, vigilantes there burned down the Paragould Cotton Compress specifically because of its employment of African Americans. In 1903, in the northeastern Arkansas counties of Cross and Poinsett, local whites belonging to the lower class of farmers, who often depended upon labor in timber and other industries to make ends meet, tried to drive off Black workers, whom their occasional employers seemed to prefer over white labor. In April 1904, the white citizens of Bonanza, a coal-mining town on the western border of the state, posted notices demanding that all

Black workers of the Central Coal and Coke Company leave the area immediately and later rioted in order to effect their departure. In March 1915, in the southeastern Arkansas city of Pine Bluff, vigilantes posted notices in a Black section of town warning residents to leave within two weeks "or suffer the penalty of death," specifically giving the motivation for the threat as: "We want your jobs."[51] (And this is to say nothing yet of how white men regarded themselves as competing against Black men for yet another finite resource—white women—and how this also motivated lynching violence. That will be covered more extensively in chapter 5, where we explore lynching in the context of mimetic theory.)

"So, when it comes to recognizing someone as a fellow human being," writes Manne, "the characteristic human capacities that you share don't just make her *relatable*; they make her potentially *dangerous* and *threatening* in ways only a human being can be—at least relative to your own distinctively human sensibilities."[52] As seen in chapter 1, whites felt threatened by the political potential of African Americans and so disfranchised them and spatially segregated society; they felt threatened by the mental potential of African Americans and so denied them schooling and threatened teachers who did dare educate Black children. And as we can see here, they felt threatened by Black labor potential, and by the eventual inability of Black Southerners to continue to absorb abuse, day after day, year after year, without rising up and ridding themselves of their tormenters. These are not the fears one feels in relation to nonhumans. An eccentric may go into the woods and preach rebellion among the opossums and the deer, openly urging them to rise up and kill humans wherever they can be found, but we would not concern ourselves that such an act bore any real potential for rebellion. But let that person take his sermons wherever oppressed peoples congregate, and the local elites would soon brand his deeds with the label of sedition.

As Manne writes, "This leaves us with an important, albeit confronting, possibility: people may know full well that those they treat in brutally degrading and inhumane ways are fellow human beings, underneath a more or less thin veneer of false consciousness. And yet, under certain social circumstances . . . they may massacre, torture, and rape them *en masse* regardless."[53] Not only that, but as we will discuss in the next chapter, they will think it a virtue to massacre, to torture, to do all the terrible things that fall under the heading of *lynching*.

4

VIRTUE

Since we cannot atone you, we shall see
Justice design the victor's chivalry.

—William Shakespeare, *Richard II*

LYNCHING CAN BE VIRTUOUS. At least, that was
the attitude of whoever wrote the opinion piece in the
Arkansas Gazette justifying the lynching of Henry James
on May 14, 1892. This piece is worth quoting in full for the
total defense of lynching presented therein:

> In the South it is the unwritten law that the
> man who commits the most atrocious of crimes
> of which a woman can be made the victim will
> die. It was in obedience to this inexorable law
> that the monster Henry James, the negro who
> so fiendishly assaulted little Maggie Doxey,
> was hanged to a telephone pole early Saturday
> morning by an infuriated mob, and riddled with
> bullets.
>
> There was no mistake in identity. The brute
> had been employed in the family to which the
> child belong [*sic*]. When arrested he confessed
> the crime, and his executioners realized that he
> deserved ten thousand deaths.
>
> It is useless to moralize, and to deplore the

reign of the mob. Every good citizen would prefer that the law should take its course. The courts are open. The flow of justice is unrestricted. In his case legal trial would have been followed by conviction, and the gallows would have claimed and found its own. But there are times when human passion becomes a law unto itself. There are times when that higher law which discards legal forms, and marches in a straight line to the execution of its awful decrees, supersedes all other tribunals, and, swift and relentless, hurls the thunderbolts of vengeance against its victims. The brute who assaulted little Maggie Doxey yielded his worthless life to this higher law. His crime was the most atrocious of all crimes; and however we may deplore the methods of the mob, who will say that he did not deserve his fate?[1]

How virtuous was this deed? So virtuous that it transcended the bounds of human legal strictures, representing a "higher law which discards legal forms." So virtuous that the representatives of this "higher law" can be equated to Zeus, king of the Olympian gods of yore, who smote his victims with thunderbolts. So virtuous that it was the only response expected for "the most atrocious of all crimes."

Henry James was described as a twenty-two-year-old "mulatto" who had been employed by the family of Charles R. Johnson of Little Rock as a general handyman for about two weeks. On the day of May 10, 1892, he reportedly raped Maggie Doxey, Johnson's five-year-old adopted daughter, while Charles Johnson and his wife were away in Hot Springs, and the only other adult in the house was Johnson's mother-in-law, one Mrs. Pennington.

After the deed, he fled on foot, and when Pennington learned what had happened, she telegraphed the Johnsons in Hot Springs, and the mayor of Little Rock, Henry Lewis Fletcher, was subsequently alerted. Detectives managed to catch Henry James by the employment of a ruse—they spread word that the Johnsons were looking to employ James for more work, apparently pretending that his alleged assault upon their daughter had not been discovered. So when James showed up at the Johnson home on the morning of May 13, he was apprehended and taken to the city jail. The mayor, however, demanded the prisoner's transfer, apparently hoping that any mob action would damage the county jail and not Little Rock's own facilities, and so there James was taken. By the time a *Gazette* reporter managed to interview the deputy sheriff who was responsible for locking James up, the sheriff and his chief deputy had already absented themselves from the scene, having heard that "a mob of a thousand men would attempt to lynch James tonight."[2]

The *Gazette*'s sensationalistic reporting on the lynching itself only serves to highlight the virtue of the deed by emphasizing the evil of Henry James. The very first lines of the report are: "Midnight! It is the hour when graveyards yawn, and hell breathes contagion to the world. It was about the hour when Henry James' guilty soul took its flight from his polluted body." When the mob arrived at the county jail and learned James was not within, some returned home, while others made their way over to the state penitentiary. There, the mob attacked the driver of a hack who, they believed, had just transferred James, until Colonel S. M. Apperson, in charge of the penitentiary at the time, met them and acknowledged that James was indeed present, and that their intended quarry would remain at the penitentiary until the morning, when he would be returned to the custody of the sheriff. As word spread about the location of Henry James, more people began arriving at the penitentiary, where various men took turns giving speeches on the nature of James's crime. The mob appealed to Apperson repeatedly to hand over James, but he refused, although he reiterated that James was to be transferred in the morning, offering the mob an apparent opportunity to seize him then. Instead, the mob decided to break down the gates to the penitentiary, which they succeeded in doing just after midnight on May 14.[3]

The mob rushed in and found James in the very first cell they came to. Interestingly, before they could hang him, one of the mob leaders called out, "No rope yet! We want to try and convict him. We want to be sure."[4] The appeal to justice may seem odd or ironic coming from a member of the lynch mob, but many lynchings did style themselves after public executions, including moments of prayer and, especially of interest to the observers, an acknowledgment of guilt on the part of the one to be executed. As the historian Amy Louise Wood has observed, "These testimonials ensured that the condemned understood his crime and punishment, an understanding that was necessary to ratify the execution as divinely sanctioned."[5] Indeed, such confessions "lent lynchings the trappings of lawful punishment and served to justify the mob's violence as rightful and warranted, despite that confessions were forced and were often obtained after the lynching was underway and not likely to be aborted."[6]

When the mob took James to the home of his reported victim, Charles Johnson, having recently returned to Little Rock, met them outside his residence and cried out, at the sight of James, "That is the man!" Moved by this statement, the mob set off in search of a good place to carry out their lynching, growing as it traveled until it numbered approximately five hundred. After ruling out several sites, the mob eventually settled in a downtown corner at the local Pythian Hall and, there, threw a rope over a telephone pole. James was provided with some time to pray and an opportunity to confess to his crime, but all he could managed was eventually to mutter, "I guess I am guilty." The mob placed a noose around his neck and strung him up, but before he was raised very high at all, the mob fired more than a hundred bullets into his body. Some of those attending the lynching included a "ladylike little woman, who occupied a seat in a carriage on one of the corners of Fifth and Main," in addition to "quite a number of gentlemen in full evening dress."

The next development further highlighted the impunity of the mob. Governor James Phillip Eagle and his wife, Mary, had just arrived in town from a visit to Memphis, Tennessee, when they saw the large crowd from their streetcar. Informed about the impending lynching, Governor Eagle bounded from the streetcar just as the first shots were fired. He was able to seize one member of the mob and started dragging him off before other men surrounded them and, after a bit of tussling, managed to free the governor's prisoner. The *Gazette* insisted that the perpetrators of this attack upon the governor (though not the lynching of James) "should be severely punished." The body of Henry James was not cut down until later in the day, after the arrival of the coroner and long after thousands of people had visited the street corner to see it hanging there (including a photographer who took pictures of the corpse).[7]

The lynching of Henry James provides an excellent example of what anthropologist Alan Page Fiske and psychologist Tage Shakti Rai have called the *theory of virtuous violence*. They summarize the theory as follows:

> When people hurt or kill someone, they usually do so because they feel they ought to: they feel that it is morally right or even obligatory to be violent. Moreover, the motives for violence generally grow out of a relationship between the perpetrator and the victim, or their relationship with third parties. The perpetrator is violent to make the relationship right—to make the relationship what it ought to be according to his or her cultural implementations of universal relational moral principles.[8]

Such a theory challenges some of our popularly held assumptions about the nature of mob violence. Lynch mobs are popularly depicted as collectives of violent irrationality, aggregates of people temporarily giving in to their basest desires—people who may regret their deeds in the days to come and perhaps feel it necessary to develop some *ex post facto* rationale for what they have done. And there may be some basis in the field of mob psychology or crowd psychology for the idea that people behave differently among large groups, especially large groups of people with whom they share significant social identities. However, Fiske and Rai argue that, far from having roots in some collective id, most violence belongs to the realm of the superego, that most violence is motivated by a sense of morality: "Virtuous violence theory is based on the observation that *people often judge that to constitute or regulate crucial relationships they are morally required to hurt or kill another person*, and that obligation makes local sociocultural sense. In other cases, violence may not be absolutely required in order to regulate important relationships, but it is condoned, praised, and admired."[9] The philosopher David Livingstone Smith likewise asserts: "The attitude of dehumanizers toward those whom they dehumanize is anything but indifferent—it's typically *highly moralistic.*"[10] Or as the literary theorist and philosopher René Girard put it, "Even the most violent persons believe that they are always reacting to a violence committed in the first instance by someone else."[11] And no matter what evils those on the receiving end experience, perpetrators of violence universally posit their actions in terms of recognized goods, according to philosopher Mikkel Thorup: "No one ever struggles for unfreedom, submission, medievalism, ignorance but for their version of freedom, independence and enlightenment."[12]

Moral action, Fiske and Rai argue, need not be exclusively something arrived at only after long contemplation, for most people "have strong, intuitive, emotional reactions to moral situations."[13] Granted, not everyone in a community will share the same morality, and some individuals may perpetrate acts of violence that are judged wrong by prevailing social norms of the time, as with, for example, mass shooters who feel themselves morally empowered to kill women; such men certainly perpetrate their violence within a moral framework, but it is not a moral framework currently shared by the relevant law enforcement agencies, mainstream media outlets, or other cultural authorities (even if they all share the same ideologies relating to gender). But collective action that goes unpunished can signify a broader shared morality, especially when that violence is widely praised.

Fiske and Rai center their theory upon relationships, arguing that the perpetrator or perpetrators employ violence in order to make a social relationship "correspond with a prescriptive model of what the relationship ought to be—what it *must* be made to be."[14] These relationships can be conceived as employing four different relational models: (1) communal sharing, (2) authority ranking, (3) equality matching, or (4) market pricing. Communal sharing centers upon support for in-group integrity, and so violence in this model might be motivated against an external threat, or even to bolster feelings of collective solidarity, as with gang-initiation rituals. Authority ranking centers upon creating or maintaining explicit hierarchies; violence in this model can be represented by the punishment of insubordination. Equality matching entails balance in relationships, a sense of reciprocity, and so manifests itself violently through the notion of eye-for-eye, tooth-for-tooth responses to real or perceived attacks. Finally, market pricing weighs the costs and benefits of various social decisions; violence in this model can be justified if deemed proportional to an initiating act or even to possible future deeds, if some overwhelming act of violence might prevent more violence down the line.[15]

We can already see the violence of lynching easily fitting Fiske and Rai's four relational models. Lynching, especially when directed at a racial other, can be employed to eliminate the threat to "our people," especially the threat to the white race that interracial relationships or alleged rape constituted (as will be explored further in chapter 5). Lynching can be employed to preserve the lower status of African Americans, especially after one of them has committed an act of resistance (as with Henry Lowery in the previous chapter) or insubordination. Lynching serves to produce a sense of reciprocity, especially as a response to murder, in which case visiting the same fate upon the killer restores balance to the community. Finally, lynching, especially as intended to terrorize the Black population of a community (explored in the first chapter), was regarded as a proportional response to ideas of inherent Black criminality and a possible means of stemming the criminal behavior of African Americans in the future.

Too, the moral motives of these four relational models "generate, shape, and preserve the social relationships a person needs in six ways": (1) creation; (2) conduct, enhancement, modulation, and transformation; (3) protection; (4) redress and rectification; (5) termination; and (6) mourning. These "constitutive phases," as Fiske and Rai call them, can be performed both nonviolently and violently and can be directed at the self, a second party, or even a third party.[16] The constitutive phases may also overlap with one another. For example, lynching as response to a reported murder serves perhaps most immediately the purpose of redress and rectification, but through the example it is meant to serve (the terror it creates), it also functions as a means of protecting the community from future harm. Lynching also can entail a mourning response, especially when the initial murder victim was reportedly well liked and perhaps even a model for others in the community.

In other words, although those undertaking lynching regarded it as a morally appropriate means of correcting or maintaining proper relationships, this did not mean that lynching entailed cold, objective justice. As noted in chapter 3, punishment can often be emotionally rewarding for the one dishing it out. As Fiske and Rai likewise observe: "We punish harm-doers when we believe that it is fundamentally just to do so and when we are morally outraged by what they have done—not when it is rational to do so in terms of preventing future harm."[17] In addition, building upon the themes of chapter 3, Fiske and Rai insist that virtuous violence cannot be based upon dehumanization, for that would negate the moral basis for violent deeds:

> We would define dehumanization as any case where we *remove* human mental capacities and emotions from people that we *previously* viewed as having those qualities in order to enable violence against them that is motivated by non-moral reasons. If violence is morally motivated, then violence is intended to regulate a relationship with a fully moral partner, against whom the perpetrator intends to inflict pain, injury, or death. There is no point in punishing or seeking revenge against a rock, tree, computer, automobile, snail, or turtle with no capacity for moral sentiments or reasoning, because they can't transgress relationships.
>
> . . . In cases of retributive punishment, morally motivated perpetrators *want* their victim to feel pain, shame, humiliation, disgrace, or the fear and horror of dying precisely because the victim was capable of thinking, intending, and planning his actions. In these cases, perpetrators are not morally disengaged; they are morally *engaged*. Victims are not dehumanized; they are *humanized*.[18]

Nowhere is this dynamic more prevalent than in the many cases in Arkansas in which the lynching victim was burned to death—for the murder of Henry Lowery, mentioned in chapter 3, was far from the only case of such a torturous mode of execution. In fact, immolation of this sort precedes even the Civil War. In 1849, two runaway slaves suspected of murdering Phillips County plantation owner Henry Yerby were tied to a tree and burned alive. As historian Kelly Houston Jones writes, "The horrific incident would have served as a reminder of the dangers inherent in running away as well as a warning of the gruesome reprisal that could result if slaves murdered their masters."[19] Burning was one way to ensure that the victim experienced the full fear and horror of dying, if only because it required significantly more preparatory work than did hanging or shooting, often with the victim to be fully aware of what awaited him.

Another early example of this in Arkansas is the burning death of Jerry Atkins in Union County—in the very southernmost part of the state—while the area was still under Union occupation. Likely a former slave, Atkins allegedly murdered two local children, Sarah K. and Jesse G. Simpson, on November 7, 1865, and then fled the county. He was captured in a nearby county and returned to the scene of his crime. According to the Goodspeed history of the area, representing oral history and family stories as captured in the 1880s and 1890s, "The citizens thought it would be but useless expense to place such a case as this in the courts, and decided to chain him to a tree and burn him. This was done November 21, all the people in the vicinity, both Black and white, assisting in his execution, which was also witnessed by a small squad of United States troops."[20] One of the troops who witnessed this lynching, George W. Lewis, described locals building a pen "of fat or pich pine split up fine. It was then set on fire in diferant places after which he lived only 3 moments & then died. After burning about 10 minutes his head & arms droped off."[21]

Another such lynching occurred in the same county

just a few years later, noteworthy for an even greater spectacle of torture. This incident is known solely from a letter, written by one Thomas Warren of Union County and published in an Arkansas newspaper, from which it was subsequently circulated throughout the country. According to this account, a pregnant white woman, left unnamed, went to a neighbor's house for a stay of several days but, finding no one home, made to return to her own abode. However, on her return, "a negro stopped her horse, took her off and drove, pushed and pulled her eight miles into the bottom lands, where he tied her to a tree and outraged her, keeping her there for three days." The report notes that she gave birth to her child while tied to the tree but does not relate its fate. The woman's husband, not finding her at the neighbor's place, went in search and found the horse and, then, his wife, dead from "blows upon the head inflicted with a club." The assailant was soon taken prisoner "by a party of negroes who were assisting in the search." And this is where things become even more horrific: "At the husband's request the negroes built two log heaps, and, setting them on fire, placed the negro between them. They were twenty-four hours burning him, and at intervals subjecting him to horrible torture, such as cutting off his toes and strips from his body."[22]

In February 1904, Glenco Bays was burned to death in Crossett in southeastern Arkansas for a murder he allegedly committed. He stood accused of killing J. D. Stephens, a prominent farmer (and deputy sheriff) on whose land he worked. Stephens, according to reports, had been having "some trouble" with Bays when "the negro went into Mr. Stephens' house, and, returning in a few seconds, fired two loads of buckshot into Mr. Stephens' breast" before striking "the dying man with the butt of the gun as he fell." Bays subsequently escaped but was captured by a posse. A dispatch from Crossett dated February 18, before Bays had been put to death, noted that a mob numbering more than a thousand had already formed "to take summary vengeance" upon Bays, adding, "Some of the mob advocate burning him."[23] According to the following day's report, Bays "made a full confession just after he was captured" and "laughed when asked how he wanted to die, saying it made no difference, as he knew full well that his hour had arrived." The mob, described as "extremely quiet" and "composed of Ashley county farmers, both black and white," then "proceeded deliberately to the task of executing the negro," agreeing "almost unanimously that he should be burned to death at the stake." So Bays was bound to a post, with brush and wood piled about him, and reportedly managed to retain "a look of defiance even in his awful suffering" as he was "slowly roasted to death." According to the *Gazette*, "The spectacle was sickening, yet not one of the witnesses appeared to doubt that the terrible punishment meted out was merited."[24]

The year 1919 saw two lynchings carried out in a similar manner. For the first, we travel back to Union County, which seems to have had an inordinate share of such murders. There, Frank Livingston was lynched on May 21, 1919. He had recently been discharged from the army at Camp Pike in central Arkansas and worked on the farm of Robinson Clay, a local farmer. According to the *Gazette*, the two men quarreled (over what is unstated), and Livingston responded by procuring an axe and killing Clay from behind. He then "walked into the house, got Mr. Clay's gun and beat Mrs. Clay to death with it" before bringing the other body into the house and lighting the residence on fire to cover his tracks. Other

African Americans, possibly employees of Clay, "rescued the charred bodies" and notified the sheriff, and a posse went in search for Livingston on the strength of a pair of bloody trousers, supposedly belonging to him, being found at the scene. The posse captured Livingston and forced a confession from him before he "was tied to a tree and burned alive."[25] In neighboring Columbia County on November 11, 1919, the first anniversary of the World War I armistice, a Black man named Jordan Jameson was similarly burned to death after allegedly murdering the local sheriff, who had shown up at Jameson's house four days prior in order to arrest him on charges of abusing his wife. Jameson shot the sheriff in the head and then fled into the nearby woods. Posses formed, including men from El Dorado in Union County, near where Livingston was killed, and local businessmen offered monetary rewards for his capture. A posse of men finally caught Jameson on the morning of November 11, but when word spread about the capture, a larger mob intercepted the posse and took Jameson for themselves. In the county seat of Magnolia, Jameson "was taken to the public square, tied to a stake, and a fire built around him. A rapidly increasing crowd witnessed the execution."[26]

As Wood asserts, for the lynch mob, "the black victim's torment offered them, and the white crowd witnessing it, a sign of their own spiritual redemption. The physical torment and tortures inflicted on the lynching victim were, in this respect, crucial elements of the white crowd's own sense of moral and spiritual superiority." For the readers of newspapers that reveled in the details of a lynching, such as the report on the murder of Henry James and the subsequent editorial justifying it, "the victim's suffering allowed them to feel their own spiritual elevation in contrast to the condemned's utter degradation.[27] Or as the philosopher Arne Johan Vetlesen writes, "Evildoing as unleashed in violent assaults against specific others never emerges qua evil, meaning qua bad, or immoral; instead it is dressed up as done for the sake of protecting the good."[28]

Even if not all lynchings were endorsed by the editorial voice of a publication, the choice of words in newspaper reports often rendered the actions of mobs or posses in stark, Manichaean terms that left no doubt about who incarnated the forces of good and who the forces of evil. Such is the case with the lynching of John Hogan. In late June 1875 in the west central Arkansas town of Dover, Russ Tucker and his son were awoken at about 4:00 a.m. due to "the screams and shrieks of one of his daughters." When he opened the door to his daughters' shared bedroom, he "found that their room had been invaded by a negro man of notoriously bad character, and that the demon had attempted to offer violence upon the person of one of his daughters." Already, the term "demon" serves to render this as a struggle between good and evil. The man fled, "pursued closely by Mr. Tucker, who soon alarmed others." However, Tucker was able to keep sight of the man and eventually captured him. After this, things took the expected turn, but the language in which the *Arkansas Gazette* presented the story makes this more than simply another encapsulation of vigilante justice, however justified:

> Quickly and silently a rope was procured and, after marching John to the woods a few hundred yards from town, he was swung up, and, after a few struggles, the life of the reckless, desperate man was ended. Thus, in less than an hour, the devilish deed attempted by this most unfortunate

> wretch brought swift retribution upon his head,
> and the rising sun found the town as quiet and
> calm as though nothing had occurred, few of the
> citizens being aware of what was going on.

What is impressive here is the obfuscating employment of passive voice: "a rope was procured," and the life of the "desperate man was ended." Here, the men whom we already know to be engaged in this act of vigilantism are rendered non-agents. Their names are even revealed at the end of the article—"H. H. Poynter, Anderson Morgan and J. Tucker"—but the *Gazette* writer nonetheless presents the murder of Hogan as something that happens to him rather than something these three men actively undertake. Too, there is reference to the "devilish deed" bringing about "swift retribution," after which the sun rises upon a community that still retains its innocence.[29]

The virtue of lynching is a theme that recurs during newspaper debates on mob violence, as, for example, with a pair of letters that appeared in the *Arkansas Gazette* in August 1898, the first from Father John Michael Lucey (mentioned in chapter 2) in response to a recent mass lynching, and the second from John W. Dickinson, a state representative from Desha County, in response to Lucey's original missive.

Lucey's complaint centered upon the August 9, 1898, lynching of five African Americans in the southeastern Arkansas town of Clarendon. The event was sensational beyond the death toll, for the five people (three men and two women) were all murdered for actions they committed at the behest of a white woman named Mabel Orr, who had been seeking a way out of her marriage to husband John Orr. Mabel managed to arrange, through her cook, Lorilla Weaver, for a local Black "conjurer" named Dennis Ricord to prepare a solution of boiled scorpions and snake heads she could use to poison John, but this proved ineffective. The women were able to recruit another Black man, Manse Castle, to shoot John Orr with a shotgun. Castle, however, backed out and passed the job off to Ricord and Will Sanders, the son of Lorilla Weaver. On his first attempt, Ricord proved unable to use the gun due to his unfamiliarity with the specific weapon. On their next attempt, Sanders was able to murder John Orr successfully through his kitchen window after he returned from choir practice. After a few days of communal bewilderment regarding the murder, the investigation zeroed in upon Mabel Orr and her accomplices, and all five were arrested, along with Orr's maid, Susie Jacobs. Orr herself, in custody, swallowed a fatal dose of poison, and as news spread that she would likely escape justice, a mob numbering in the hundreds formed outside the jail, overpowered authorities, and lynched the remaining five people implicated in the crime.

The *Arkansas Gazette*, in a departure from previous editorial stances, condemned the lynching in Clarendon without even offering the typical statement of understanding, of sympathy with the people who carried out the murder: "It is a terrible blot on Clarendon. It is an awful record for law-abiding Monroe County. It is a black spot on the state's history which can never be effaced."[30] Indeed, the fact that two women were lynched seemed especially to provoke condemnation, but as historian Richard Buckelew, author of the definitive treatment on this event, has written, "While it might seem unusual and particularly barbaric to lynch the two black women involved, the fact that they were involved in poisoning their employer touched a nerve in the white community. The fear of poisoning by black servants was a long-held fear of whites who employed them."[31]

In its August 18, 1898, issue, the *Gazette* published

a missive from Father Lucey commending the paper for its unequivocating stance regarding the mob violence in Clarendon, stating, "Every thoughtful citizen of the state must shudder at the outrage. Such an affair, if viewed as an index of our civilization, and it has become such in being one of a lengthy series, places the United States below Mexico in the grade of nations." The priest then went on to highlight "two capital offenses which strike at the root of political life," namely "lawless taking of human life and corruption of the ballot box," adding that, in the South, tracing "these evils to their source is to come to the negro." For Lucey, the "endless trouble" that seemed to mark "the relations of the white and negro races" was marked by a devolution of the idea of justice: "At first, only rape was to be visited by lynching; next murder was added, and now any exciting crime will do; for we come to the negro." Further down Lucey actually recommends that federal courts take over the administration of law "if state courts cannot deal with crimes between whites and negroes," though admitting that such a course "may not be feasible."

Lucey's letter demonstrates the difficulty of arguing against lynching from the context of a "race relations" approach to matters of justice and human rights—attempting to do so riddles his arguments with inconsistencies. For example, he seems to locate the impetus for lynching not with structural inequalities as relating to the respective power of each group, but rather with poor representatives of both races: "The negro question has been settled many times, but never justly. It must be taken out of the hands of the two worst elements of both races, 'the white trash' and the 'fool nigger.'" He then suggests the necessity of "an education, industrial as well as literary, and moral as well as political" being provided for African Americans to prepare them to "enjoy the franchise and become a real American citizen," without any comparable program of improvement for the people he has already dubbed "the white trash"—and despite the fact that he later insists that "everyone who took an active part in the lynching," not just the lower element of the white race, "is a murderer and legally all such are subject to indictment, conviction and death." However, Lucey does issue one clear call to end the hypocrisy of the present regime: "If the negro is not to enjoy the franchise, let the proclamation be openly made. The evils arising from the corruption of the ballot to defeat the negro are already very serious. The violations of the law are grave."[32] Granted, Lucey does not directly state that empowering African Americans politically is the best way to end lynching and, instead, holds lynching and the "corruption of the ballot box" to be equivalent assaults upon constitutional rule, but his readers may well have made the connection in their own right.

Eight days later, the *Gazette* published a missive by Representative Dickinson, who stated that Lucey's own writing had created "the impression that he loves the negro so well he is willing to put 'black heels upon white necks.'" Furthermore, the legislator explicitly linked the prevalence of lynching to the prevalence of crimes warranting it: "Judge Lynch does not hold his court in Arkansas more frequently than he does in the other states of the Union, or in the civilized world where the brutal crimes of rape and assassination occur—nor does he legislate against color—and if the negro gets into his court more often it is because he commits these crimes more frequently. This fact anybody knows." Then, in order to underscore the apparent virtue—or at least necessity—of lynching, Dickinson cites unnamed representatives of both the law and the clergy:

A great barrister has well said: "The history of the civilized world does not record one solitary instance in which a man has been punished for defending the virtue of his mother, his sister, his wife or his kinswoman." If this be true, and we believe it is, then we conclude that when such crimes as were recently perpetrated at Clarendon and in Grant county are committed, the whole people become temporarily insane and call into operation Judge Lynch's court.

A great bishop said in substance in speaking of the lynching of the brute that ravished and killed the four-year-old girl at Texarkana a few years since: "If it had been my little girl that had thus been treated, I am not sure but that I would have become insane as that whole community was at that time, and done the lynching myself." A crime committed by a man whilst he is insane is not punishable, and doubtless juries, grand and petit, have such cases which they discharge upon this proposition. Arkansas is not more in the habit of lynching than any other state or country, and ought not to be abused as she has been by many writers.[33]

In other words, men become insane in response to the occurrence of certain evils, but this state of insanity can be regarded as one in which men ably defend the virtues of women. Too, the reference to "the civilized world" and other countries is designed to put Arkansas on a moral equivalency with more elevated and ancient societies; recall in the previous chapter how the lynchers in Stuttgart considered their deed in a positive light compared to a recent official execution in England. Besides, the "great" barristers and bishops essentially endorsed as understandable, as natural, the state of temporary insanity that arises from the desire or necessity to defend one's womenfolk. And if these states of violent insanity are typically directed against "the negro," it is because that race commits a greater number of crimes and thus deserves more punishment.

Even when a newspaper might argue against the act of lynching, it could sometimes do so by reference to a greater suffering available to the would-be victim. On the night of October 16, 1911, Nathan Lacey was lynched in Forrest City in northeastern Arkansas for having allegedly "attempted to assault Mrs. Thomas Cox." After his arrest, a mob of some three hundred men arrived at the county jail and overpowered the sheriff before breaking down the doors of the building, and then the door to Lacey's cell, with sledgehammers. According to the *Arkansas Democrat*, the mob then dragged Lacey from the building by a rope around his neck and marched him for about a mile to a local brickyard, where "the negro shrieked and begged for his life, praying to his God for mercy and to his captors for time to prepare to meet his fate." The mob then, with the stereotypically reported "quiet," hanged Lacey from the cross arm of a telegraph pole, where the body remained hanging until the following morning. The *Gazette*, however, reported that the mob hanged Lacey briefly and then let him down "in order that he might make a statement or utter a prayer" before pulling him "up by the neck" and leaving him there. The latter newspaper took pains to emphasize the reputable behavior of the mob: "The mob was not a riotous one. There was no drinking and not a shot was fired by any member of it."[34]

The *Arkansas Democrat* reflected upon the lynching of Nathan Lacey in an editorial that attempts to present lynching as the lesser or two alternatives for stemming the criminal nature of "negro brutes." While it could not argue against lynching without reinforcing the notion that a righteous cause lay behind so many mob murders, as well as indirectly crediting lynching as efficient and representative of the democratic spirit, it did present the trappings of "law and order" as a means of fostering a greater sense of existential dread in the Black population as a whole. Titled "Do Lynchings Pay?" it is worth quoting in full:

> Does the lynching of a man accomplish any good? That is a question that the people have been asking for years past and the answer appears to be as uncertain and indefinite today as it was in the past century when the first lynchings were heard of in this country.
>
> There are two ways of looking at lynchings— from the abstract and from the concrete. From the former there is no doubt that no good is accomplished. Take, for instance, the lynching of Nathan Lacey at Forrest City, Monday night.
>
> The black brute attempted to assault the wife of a prominent farmer of St. Francis County. He was chased down and captured and placed in jail. There is practically no doubt that he would have been convicted and legally executed.
>
> Would not the trying of this negro and the legal hanging of the fiend accomplish more than the wreaking of summary vengeance upon him by a gathering of 300 men without warrant of law?
>
> But the other side.
>
> The husband of the woman who was attacked, his relatives and her kinsmen and the close personal friends of the family are to

be taken into consideration. What would be the feeling of these people toward the human monstrosity that had entered the home and attempted to do violence to the wife and mother?

That they should have desired the life of Nathan Lacey is easy to understand.

But there is nothing to show that any of those people were members of the mob that hanged the negro. Therefore it devolves upon other residents of St. Francis County. They were probably acquaintances of the husband whose home had been entered. They were possibly fired by the thought that should the negro be allowed to live another might attempt a similar assault upon some of their loved ones. Therefore, it is easy to argue, they executed him as a warning to any man who might contemplate such a deed.

But is it a warning? Does the lynching of a negro have any salutary effect upon others of their race who might contemplate such an act?

It is very doubtful. The negro who is guilty of an attack on a woman is ninety-nine cases out of every hundred the man who has little or no education, who is possessed only of the lowest sort of intelligence and who is really more brute than man.

It is usually the case that the negro guilty of such an act is incapable of reasoning out the principle of cause and effect to the extent of applying it to his own case.

But when a negro is imprisoned for several months, perhaps, given a fair and impartial trial, condemned to death and hanged for his crime, the fact is discussed throughout the countryside. Even the most ignorant acquire more or less information regarding the crime itself, the trial and conviction, and the horrible thought of waiting behind steel bars for that hour to come when his fellowman has decreed he shall die to pay the penalty for his infringement of God and man-made law, weighs more or less heavily upon even the poor mentality of the average black.

It is easy for those who have not had the fiend to come into their own home, to preach moderation, and it should be done for the general effect it may have, but it accomplishes about as much with the near relatives of the victim as the singing of Psalms does with the dead mule.

But to those who take part in these summary executions, it should become a matter of serious consideration.

Do lynchings pay?[35]

What the editorial author attempts here is very interesting. He asserts that, from the abstract perspective, "there is no doubt that no good is accomplished," given that the person in question would have been hanged anyway, but he does acknowledge that lynchings can have a salutary effect for those most closely connected to the alleged precipitating act—in this case, the attempted assault. However, the editorialist also tries to argue for the greater virtue of letting the law work its course by appealing to a sense of humanist violence, as covered in chapter 3. The law, in this case, would inspire greater dread (and thus serve as a better corrective) precisely because it draws out the suffering of the man convicted, and thus inspires greater sympathetic suffering on the part of all who can identify with the convict by virtue of shared racial identity. A lynching, in other words, ends a life too quickly to serve as an example.

Only the law can act virtuously enough to resonate with the humanity of "the average black" as a collective.

In short, those who lynched imagined themselves committing deeds of high virtue. And those who opposed lynching often cast their opposition in the light of greater pain and suffering for not only the victim himself but also for the entire Black community, and such pain and suffering would itself be virtuously undertaken. But what is truly interesting is that even those opposing lynching could sometimes, strategically, evoke the virtues of actual violence. For example, *The Appeal* of St. Paul, Minnesota, a Black newspaper, editorialized thusly on the lynching of James, covered at the beginning of this chapter, to interrogate the broader system of white supremacy in the United States, asking such questions as the following:

> Does any fair-minded person suppose there was any actual desire on the part of the authorities to prevent the mob at Little Rock, Ark., from breaking into the penitentiary and taking therefrom Henry James the Afro-American accused of outraging the little white girl last week? The guards in that penitentiary could have kept a mob of 10,000 at bay for an indefinite period.
>
> Does any fair-minded person believe that had Henry James been white and Maggie Doxey black and the circumstances otherwise exactly the same that there would have been any such exhibition in the defence of outraged virtue by the "superior race"?
>
> Would a black Maggie Doxey at five years of age been any less pure than a white one?
>
> Would an assault on a black virgin five years

old by a letcherous [*sic*] white brute been any less aggravating than if the colors were reversed?

Did anybody ever hear of a white mob lynching a white man for outraging a black virgin?

Why cannot a black man be tried in the legal courts? If there is any doubt of his innocense [*sic*] he will get the benefit of the doubt.

Would it not be following the first law of nature if the constantly outraged Afro-Americans take "Lex talionis" as their motto all over the South, and act in accordance with the motto?

If an insurrection a thousand-fold greater than the Nat Turner insurrection should break out in the South who would be to blame?[36]

SCAPEGOAT

Hear me, sympathetic gods,
pay the debt of past bloodshed
with this just, fresh slaughter.

—Aeschylus, *The Libation Bearers*[1]

"WAS LYNCHED FOR ELOPING" ran the headline in the July 7, 1905, issue of the *Arkansas Democrat*, followed by "Negro Meets Death at Dumas for Running Away with White Girl." The man in question was apparently named Joe Woodman—or, at least, a letter addressed to one Joe Woodman of Rives, Arkansas, was found in his pocket by the coroner's jury after the fact. According to the report, suspicions arose when this apparent Woodman, who worked at a sawmill near Rives in Drew County, located in southeastern Arkansas, "disappeared from his home" at the same time as did the sixteen-year-old daughter of a white man, J. S. Small, who lived in the same neighborhood. After investigations were undertaken, authorities heard from several witnesses who had seen the couple "on the northbound local train." These authorities contacted the sheriff at Pine Bluff, to the north, and he managed to pull the couple off the train at the small town of Tamo and send them back down on the southbound local. As might be imagined, Woodman was met at the depot in Dumas "by a crowd of men, who seemed to be from the vicinity of Rives, bent on trouble." Law enforcement managed to get him to the jail, but as the *Democrat* reported, "Every place of business closed early and quiet reigned supreme during the night."[2]

That night, a crowd of men visited the jail and "proceeded to carry out its purpose quietly," according to the *Arkansas Gazette*. They broke into the jail, and "the negro was taken out and marched to a point on the railroad track half a mile south of town and there he was hanged from a telegraph pole. There was no disturbance of the slumbers of Dumas' citizens." And the report closes with these lines: "The lynching has created no great excitement in this vicinity and no arrests have occurred in connection with the affair. So far as known not a citizen of Dumas was in the crowd nor was connected in any way with the act."[3]

This was not the first elopement-related lynching in the state of Arkansas. For example, a brief story in the October 4, 1887, issue of the *Gazette* reported the lynching of one Oscar Jeffries for the same deed in Sevier County in southwestern Arkansas. According to this report, Jeffries was "a fine looking young colored man from Oswego, N.Y." who had traveled to that corner of Arkansas "to take charge of a colored academy there." Following his arrival, he began to pay "considerable attentions" to Ina W. Jones, "daughter of one of the largest plantation owners in the counties"— and a white girl. Jones herself was apparently taken with Jeffries and, "despite the entreaties and threats of her parents" regarding the relationship, told friends that she intended to marry the man. Once her parents heard this, they "locked the girl in her chamber." As anyone familiar with this trope from romances might well predict, this did not hinder the lovers: "Despite these precautions Jeffries got a ladder and during the night entered the room where Miss Jones was sleeping. He aroused her and they left for an adjoining hamlet, where they were married early next morning." The girl's father formed a posse and managed to overtake the couple in the evening, and Jeffries was "riddled with bullets, over thirty balls lodging in his body." Ina Jones was taken home, and according to the newspaper account, proved "glad Jeffries was killed, as she was infatuated with him, and only awoke to her condition when she found she had actually married a black man."[4] Of course, we readers may wonder about such a statement, since she must have known that the man leading the local "colored academy" was not white, and if the words are her own, what other choice might she have had but to give in?

Of course, many lynchings were justified by reference to the myth of the "Black beast rapist," and, as will be discussed below, some men lynched due to allegations of rape were likely in consensual relationships with white women. So it rather stands out that Arkansas newspapers openly acknowledged that Jeffries and Woodman were lynched for eloping with white women. In these reports, there is no hint that either man in any way exercised his will over his lover, that they forced them into marriage or did anything more dishonorable, for the time period, other than sneaking away to marry without parental permission. But these men were Black, and that made all the difference. The mob would have punished them for rape had that been an excuse they could have used, but they were just as happy to punish them for love.

The same was likely true for Robert Hicks, an African American man in his early twenties, who was lynched on November 23, 1921, near Lake Village in the southeastern-most corner of Arkansas. His crime, as relayed by the

Arkansas Gazette, was thus: "Hicks is said to have written an insulting letter to an 18-year-old Lake Village girl." The word "insulting" here is ambiguous, but like such words as *outrage* or *assault* often employed to describe a range of supposed misdeeds, from simple propositioning to outright rape, the nature of the alleged "insult" can depend rather heavily upon the racial identity of the person delivering the message. After all, Emmett Till was lynched in 1955 for having "insulted a white woman" when he reportedly asked Carolyn Bryant for a date. A compliment delivered by the wrong person could be an insult.

And the further actions of Hicks argue for this interpretation, for after sending his missive, "he appeared at the young woman's home, and asked her if she had received his letter." But by then, news of his letter had circulated, and he "was apprehended by several Lake Village men when he appeared at the young woman's home." These men took him to a point four miles from town and riddled his body with bullets. It was found the next day, and the coroner's inquest concluded that "Hicks came to his death at the hands of persons unknown," as was typical.[5]

What lies at the center of each of these cases of lynching is a conflict over desire—or, at least, in the case of Hicks, an apparent attribution of desire to the eventual victim. Allegations of interracial rape tended to dominate lynching discourse in the late nineteenth and early twentieth centuries, often serving as a cover, as Ida B. Wells discovered, for conflicts personal or economic. However, there is not even the hint that rape or any associated form of violence provided motivation for the lynchings just mentioned. In fact, the state newspapers of the time, which rarely hesitated to provide a more noble reason for the murder of a "negro miscreant" should one be hinted at, were forced to acknowledge that in desire, not any accusation of violence, lay the genesis of these particular crimes.

To say that these lynchings were rooted in desire is not to say that Black men were lynched for desiring white women, for that would invite a corollary statement to the effect that, if Black men wished to cease being lynched, then they should cease desiring white women. In fact, many politicians, preachers, and newspapers said as much during the late nineteenth and early twentieth centuries—that it was Black desire for love or lust beyond the bounds of race that drove the fury of the mob. This idea ran so deep that it was often internalized by Black communities themselves. For example, on August 18, 1899, the Central District Baptist Association, a Black Baptist group, passed a resolution "condemning and discountenancing the crime of rape" which specifically linked its efforts to combat rape with its advocacy against lynching, as stated at the end: "Resolved, That we compliment and thank the public press for its most effective work against the crime of lynching and that in turn we feel called upon to rally and work just as effectively to reduce and annihilate the rape record in this country."[6]

However, publicly stated efforts to combat sexual crimes would not reduce the frequency with which African American men were associated with those crimes, very often by the media and government officials themselves. As Governor Jeff Davis said during an October 25, 1905, visit to Little Rock by President Theodore Roosevelt, "Charitable and indulgent as we have ever been to an inferior race . . . if the brutal criminals of that race . . . lay unholy hands upon our fair daughters, nature is so riven and shocked that the dire compact produces social cataclysm, often, in its terrific sweep, far beyond the utmost counter efforts of all civil power." Davis also publicly said that he would prefer to bury his daughter alive than to see her "arm in arm with the best nigger on earth," so it is not merely violence that invites the cataclysm, but the racial identities of those brought to union (after all, if he would prefer to bury his daughter alive, we can well imagine what he would prefer to do to her suitor).[7] At the same time, though, many public thinkers insisted that it was natural for Black people to long for romances with white people, given the superiority exhibited by the white race and the opportunity for Black people, thereby, to produce mixed children and thus "elevate" their own stock. According to this logic, then, Black men were being lynched for exhibiting the characteristics of Black men. But the fear of interracial relationships perhaps went deeper than a concern over the safety of white women. As the historian Philip Dray writes, "Compounding the white man's certainty that black men desired white women was the gnawing possibility that white women desired black men. This made it necessary not only to despise and criminalize the black male but also to make him subhuman, a monkey man, to desexualize him and remove him altogether from the sphere of the white woman's sexual choices."[8]

Lynching was but one means of removing the Black man from the sphere of white women's sexual choices, for laws against interracial marriage had been on the books since the earliest days of statehood. For example, in 1837, the year following Arkansas's transition from territory to state, the legislature passed a law declaring void "all marriages between white persons and Negroes or mulattos," even if "it did not prescribe a specific punishment for violators," as historian Charles F. Robinson has written.[9] This law did not actually outlaw interracial sex—only marriage. The state also legislated the death penalty for a conviction of rape, and this pertained even to slaves, despite the fact that they were the property of another. However, historian Kelly Houston Jones has reviewed a variety of antebellum Arkansas trials in which a slave stood accused of attempting to rape a white woman, some of which were even appealed to the state Supreme Court, and concluded that even though accusations of attempted rape could trigger a lynching in the post–Civil War period, such charges "did not cause much mob action in antebellum Arkansas," which demonstrated "relatively uneventful public reaction to rape accusations."[10] And this dynamic was present in other parts of the South. As Dray has written, "In cases of alleged rape, records suggest that antebellum courts, again because of the value of slave property, proceeded with relative restraint, and were even occasionally nuanced enough in their rulings to acknowledge that some black-white sexual relationships were consensual, a finding that would be unthinkable fifty years later."[11] No doubt, the totalitarian control already exercised through the institution of slavery mitigated the need to terrorize those who allegedly transgressed racial boundaries in such a fashion. In fact, according to historian Diane Miller Sommerville, the efficacy of charges of rape against slaves in the antebellum era could depend largely upon the character of the person making the accusation:

> Although rape laws unequivocally spelled out harsh penalties for black men who sexually assaulted white females, some white female accusers had an easier time than others in convincing juries of the truthfulness of their

claims and seeing their alleged rapists punished to the fullest extent of the law. Poorer females were more likely than wealthier females to face a hostile courtroom and dubious white community. Females without male protectors appear to have been treated more shabbily than those with fathers, husbands, or other male kin acting on their behalf. And women who deviated from accepted sexual codes of behavior could find themselves as much on trial as their alleged attackers.[12]

The idea of interracial rape (at least, the rape of white women by Black men) as the most frightful crime that could be committed would not emerge until after the Civil War.

While a Unionist government under Isaac Murphy was formed in 1864, during the tail end of the Civil War, conservative Arkansas Democrats were able to regain power in 1866, prior to the advent of Congressional Reconstruction, and among the laws they enacted was a replica of the antebellum law against interracial marriage. With the imposition of Congressional Reconstruction the following year, Arkansans were required once again to develop a new state constitution. During the 1868 constitutional convention, one delegate, John M. Bradley of Bradley County, introduced a resolution calling for the prohibition of marriage between Blacks and whites. As Robinson writes, "Although Bradley's proposal probably reflected his heartfelt opposition to interracial marriage, his primary objective may have been to fracture the fragile unity that existed between white Republicans of northern and southern origin (the so-called carpetbaggers and scalawags, respectively), the southerners being understood to be more conservative on racial matters."[13] During the debate, William H. Grey, a Black delegate from the cotton-rich Phillips County in eastern Arkansas, rose to say:

> I know that such provisions have heretofore more or less obtained; but while the contract has been kept on our part, it has not been kept upon the part of our friends; and I propose, if such an enactment is inserted in the Constitution, to insist, also, that if any white man shall be found cohabitating with a negro woman, the penalty shall be death.[14]

Grey dared to speak the unspoken truth that white men were much more likely to have sex with Black women (whether consensual or not) than Black men were to have sex with white women. It was a daring speech that acknowledged a truth made invisible by the rhetoric and fear of white Southerners—the real nature of the "mulatto" population. After all, if, as noted above, a Black male slave attempting to rape a white woman during those antebellum years rarely led to a lynching, said slave was nonetheless punished in some way. But not punished were those white masters who, generation after generation, had availed themselves of the bodies of their enslaved women, producing a "mulatto" population that, on the verge of the Civil War, was threatening to become a region-wide scandal—as well as threatening to undermine the nature of racial classification itself (as discussed briefly in chapter 1). As historian Joel Williamson notes:

> The increasing mulatto population was a profound indictment of the biracial Southern system. In the South's ideal world, all slaves were black and all blacks were slaves. Further,

the black as slave was locked into place as the perfect complement to the white as free. A rising rage for identity among whites left increasingly little room for a blurring of the color line, and a civilization on the make took great pains to blind itself to the whiteness of its mulatto children. The white world tried to ignore mulattoes, but mulattoes repaid that attempted neglect with an intense scrutiny of the white world and, generally, with that best form of flattery—imitation. Mulattoes usually knew who were their white fathers and mothers, and they were led by their society often to value their lighter color and to relish the culture that it represented.[15]

So for Grey to refer to the true nature of interracial sex in the South, and then to demand the death penalty for any white man who sought sex across racial boundaries, was quite the challenge to the sensibilities of those attempting to recreate antebellum divisions in Arkansas.

After Radical Republicans voted to shunt a proposal on miscegenation off to a committee for further study, the *Arkansas Gazette* opined:

The vote was understood to be a test, and the result shows that the radical party of Arkansas favor social equality for the negro and the intermarriage of the races. White men of Arkansas! can you longer affiliate with the advocates of miscegenation and mongrelism? The leader of the radical party in the brindled assemblage says he wants no constitutional provision to prevent a negro from marrying into his family. Do you endorse this? If not, come out from among the champions of mongrelism and join the great white man's party of Arkansas.[16]

In the end, all the convention could pass on the subject was a resolution opposing "all amalgamation." However, as historian Paul C. Palmer has written, the various speeches "lead one to suspect that not everyone in the convention viewed miscegenation as the most heinous of crimes. But even in that revolutionary conclave, no one possessed the temerity to defend it."[17] Although the antebellum ban on interracial marriage technically remained on the books, it seems to have been largely ignored, with the *Arkansas Gazette* reporting, and census records revealing, a number of interracial marriages from 1868 onward.[18]

However, as the 1868 constitutional convention exposed, conservatives typically aligned with the Democratic Party were more than willing to use the idea of interracial relationships as a wedge issue to try to separate the Republican leadership from its new body of Black voters while also unifying white Southerners under the banner of race. As noted above, white unity during the antebellum years could be rather loose, with white women in rape trials typically judged on the basis of their class standing. Too, white society was often fractured along the lines of slave ownership, which could breed resentment on the part of those who owned no slaves, as we saw in chapter 3 with the efforts of the Mechanics Institute of Little Rock to limit the types of labor slaves could undertake. After the Civil War, with former slaves enfranchised and the primacy of the Democratic Party no longer a given in the South, the old planter elite sought to quash dissension by rallying the white citizenry around the banner of race— an expansion of the collective racial "self" to ward off the influence of the increasingly racialized "other." This meant an expansion, too, of the respectability of race; as the sociologist Mattias Smångs notes, "While white women of the elite planter classes had personified the antebellum slave

South itself, the conflation of white womanhood with the idea of the white South was in the wake of the Civil War broadened to include all white women." This broadening invested "the interracial sexual boundary with previously unknown symbolic sacredness that conferred meaning to whites as a racial group."[19] And the sacralization of all white women desacralized all Black men, making of them potential rapists and making any assault upon any white women the worst of crimes that could be committed. What Ashraf H. A. Rushdy calls the "lynching for rape" discourse "allows lynchers and their advocates to claim the high ground of justice, chivalry, and morality"—in other words, to claim the greatest virtues of white manhood. Thus, opposing lynching could be interpreted as "being against chivalry, against family, against the rights of self-defense, against morality, against virtually everything decent."[20]

As noted in chapter 2, the 1890s saw the emergence of mandated spatial segregation in Arkansas, combined with efforts at disfranchising African Americans. In 1895, the Arkansas Supreme Court ruled in *Dodson v. State*, a case arising from the arrest of an interracial couple in Pulaski County in central Arkansas, that the state's 1866 marriage law should be considered as still in force. In 1911, the state legislature went even further with Act 320, which banned not simply marriage but also interracial cohabitation. As Robinson notes, state authorities were largely reluctant to enforce state laws against miscegenation, with the state Supreme Court reversing a number of convictions on that count.[21] However, vigilantes would sometimes fill in for the absent state to ensure that the color line was being well patrolled. For example, in late April 1894, Louis White, a Black resident of Brandywine Island on the Arkansas side of the Mississippi River, was visited by whitecappers Hess

Colbert, Will and Babe Jett, and John and Joe Rast, who suspected the Black man of entertaining visits from "a white widow." Colbert and the Jett brothers entered White's house, and "White fired on the intruders with a Winchester, killing Colbert." The woman in question was not found in his company, "and this fact saved White from being lynched." He was, however, arrested and charged with murder.[22]

But this newspaper report also frames the interracial relationship as mutual—the white woman was visiting the Black man, and the band of vigilantes showed up at his place expecting to find her. And it bears repeating that, although he murdered one of these vigilantes in self-defense, he would not be lynched because the woman suspected of visiting him, suspected of being in a consensual relationship of some kind with this Black man, was not found on the premises. Joe Woodman, meanwhile, would not be spared, despite his lack of violent resistance, precisely because his white bride-to-be was found with him. In fact, the possible discovery of a relationship between a Black man and white woman may have resulted in what journalist and anti-lynching activist Ida B. Wells described as one of "the most shocking and repulsive" murders she had ever documented—the lynching of Ed Coy in Texarkana, in the very southwestern corner of Arkansas.[23]

But before we proceed to that lynching, we need to explore further the linkage between desire and violence beyond the reputed desire of Black men for white women that justified so much legal and extralegal activity, for it is in understanding how desire leads to violence in general that we can begin to comprehend exactly why any hint of romance across racial boundaries constituted such a cataclysmic threat to white society in the American South.

The primary cultural theory locating the origin

of violence in desire is René Girard's mimetic theory, which takes its name from the Greek work *mimesis*, meaning mimicry or imitation. As theologian Wolfgang Palaver states, mimesis "is a fundamental part of man's constitution—and not merely an external addition to an essentially autonomous being."[24] This fact can be seen in how children acquire language, for example. But imitation is not limited to "just visual and more tangible realities of shared actions and gestures," according to psychologist Scott R. Garrels: "In tandem with these physical markers are internal mental states such as desires, beliefs, intentions, goals, which help predict and explain human actions. These internal states are what provide purpose and meaning to our actions in the world and in our social relationships."[25] Or as Girard writes in his groundbreaking volume *Violence and the Sacred*:

> Once his basic needs are satisfied (indeed, sometimes even before), man is subject to intense desires, though he may not know precisely for what. The reason is that he desires *being*, something he himself lacks and which some other person seems to possess. The subject thus looks to that other person to inform him of what he should desire in order to acquire that being. If the model, who is apparently already endowed with superior being, desires some object, that object must surely be capable of conferring an even greater plentitude of being. It is not through words, therefore, but by the example of his own desire that the model conveys to the subject the supreme desirability of the object.[26]

In short, human beings learn what to desire by imitating other people. This, however, can lead to conflict. "Rivalry," writes Girard, "does not arise because of the fortuitous convergence of two desires on a single object; rather, *the subject desires the object because the rival desires it*. In desiring an object the rival alerts the subject of the desirability of the object."[27]

According to Girard, "In human relationships words like *sameness* and *similarity* evoke an image of harmony. If we have the same tastes and like the same things, surely we are bound to get along. But what will happen when we have the same desires?"[28] As philosopher Kate Manne writes, "The more similar others are to ourselves, the more one may have to watch out for them, in the case of competing claims or interests."[29] And these competing claims lie at the core of the violence that follows, for the model suddenly finds himself a competitor for the object of his desire; he ends up feeling betrayed by his disciple/rival, who in turn feels betrayed or rejected by the sudden appearance of scorn on the part of the model. In fact, the rival can end up serving as the model of desire as the desires of the two begin to reflect one another's. This rivalry can lead to violence, and the use of this violence becomes connected mentally with the original desire, so that violence is seen as the means of attaining the ultimate goal.

What Girard calls *mimetic desire* serves as the source of tremendous social crisis that threatens the entire community. This crisis can come to the fore especially in those situations where intimate human relationships stand at the center. As Palaver writes, "Sexual desire is one of the human passions that can very easily produce situations in which two people fight over an object that cannot be shared."[30] However, there are ways of mitigating effects of mimetic desire. One is a rigid social hierarchy that keeps large numbers of potential rivals rooted in their lower positions, thus reducing the threat of potential equality. "As long as social difference or any other form of differentiation is present to channel mimetic desire, its conflictual dimension remains contained," writes Palaver.[31] Thus, as he notes, social transformations that equalize the relative class or status positions of formerly unequal groups of people can foster conflict by facilitating mimetic rivalry: "As the metaphysical distance between desiring subject and model diminishes—the key component of internal mediation—the potential for rivalry and violence increases. The more negligible this distance becomes, the more probable it is that mimesis will end in rivalry and violence."[32]

This was, of course, the situation in the late nineteenth and early twentieth centuries in Arkansas and in the United States (and world) as a whole, when social transformations were threatening once rigid hierarchies—even without considering the relative position of racial groups. As international security expert Michael Brown writes:

> The process of economic development, the advent of industrialization, and the introduction of new technologies, it is said, bring out a wide variety of profound social changes: migration and urbanization disrupt existing family and social systems and undermine traditional political institutions; better education, higher literacy rates, and improved access to growing mass media raise awareness of where different people stand in society. At a minimum, this places strain on existing social and political systems. It also raises economic and political expectations, and can lead to mounting frustration when these expectations are not met. This can be particularly problematic in the political realm, because demands for political participation usually outpace the ability of systems to respond.[33]

Such post–Civil War transformations would have been enough to disturb residents of the South. Now, add in the fact that the emancipation of slaves—and the enfranchisement of former slaves—decreased the rigidly enforced metaphysical difference between Black and white far more than did the prevalence of "mulattoes," whose existence, at least, was typically predicated upon patterns of sexual exploitation and thus aligned in spirit with the privileges reserved for those atop the hierarchy. Furthermore, as noted in chapter 3, these former slaves and their descendants could be construed as competition for scarce jobs and resources with those whites who used to be so far above them on the Great Chain of Being. So when they were able, with the end of Reconstruction and the launch of political "Redemption," Southern whites turned their attention toward campaigns of disfranchisement and segregation, as mentioned in chapter 2. Lynching was a part of this. As religious studies professor Donald G. Mathews argues, "The difference between enslaving, segregating, and disfranchising African Americans and torturing them to death is a difference of degree, not a difference of kind."[34] The difference between forbidding interracial cohabitation and/or marriage and lynching the Black husband of a newlywed white woman was, likewise, a difference of degree.

As Girard writes, "Unlike animal rivalries, these imitative or mimetic rivalries can become so intense and contagious that not only do they lead to murder but they spread, mimetically, to entire communities."[35] We have seen how the law can be employed to solve the issue of mimetic desire by enforcing rigid hierarchies and the separation of groups. But lynching also played an important role. The profusion of mimetic rivalries can threaten the very foundations of communal order, and equanimity can only be restored through the focusing of violent desire upon a surrogate victim, a scapegoat, whose elimination or expulsion allows the community to survive. As philosopher Arne Johan Vetlesen summarizes:

> The atmosphere is such that outbursts of violence seem imminent: there thus arises a need to channel the urge to violence beyond the boundaries of a community, since within it violence is prohibited. So, instead of representing a threat against the group's future, violence is "recycled" into the chief weapon defending the unity of the group.... The purpose of the sacrifice is to restore harmony within the community and to reinforce integration: the group is confirmed as unison and homogenous, the identity of the members is confirmed as unequivocally linked with the group.[36]

But only certain individuals are useful for purposes of sacrifice or scapegoating. As Girard notes, community members "are less suitable as ritual victims than are nonmembers," for the purpose is to unify the community around the elimination of an "other." However, neither can the scapegoat be entirely foreign to the community in question, for then he cannot represent what the community needs to eliminate or expel, being already and always exterior to the group in question. "Rather," writes Girard, the ideal scapegoat is a "monstrous double": "He partakes of all possible differences within the community, particularly the difference between within and without; for he passes freely from the interior to the exterior and back again. ... The victim must be neither too familiar to the community nor too foreign to it."[37] According to Vetlesen:

> In order to fulfil its integrative function the candidate surrogate victim needs to appear as possessing a semblance with subversive or erosive elements *within* the community, a semblance that is of precisely *appropriate* degree to serve as a warning, thus ensuring that these elements "take the hint" and remain at their proper place within the community. In this way, each and everyone "inside" can prove their belongingness for all to see by joining in the violent ritual sacrifices directed at specific objects outside the community. Since the objects chosen will enjoy no established relationships with the "legitimate" members of the community, the violence can be enacted with impunity and without risk of retaliation.[38]

Vetlesen, who applies a Girardian analysis to genocidal violence in the former Yugoslavia in his 2005 book *Evil and Human Agency*, concludes that such collective violence "is always seen to be a deliberate action carried out *for the sake of* protecting some superior yet threatened 'good'—i.e. the unity and cohesion of the group, especially at times of crisis for the group, a crisis often sensed as—or rather, by group leaders *presented* as—putting the sheer *survival* of the group into question."[39] Once the violence has been committed, however, "a feeling of collective reconciliation is engendered throughout the mob," according to Palaver. "The monstrosity of the preceding crisis is now manifested in one single monster; we are dealing with one victim, which has become the scapegoat for the entire community.[40]

"AT THE STAKE" was the first-page headline of the February 21, 1892, issue of the *Arkansas Gazette*, beneath which were the words, "Edward Coy, the Assailant of

Mrs. Henry Jewell, Atones for the Crime."[41] And how did he atone for the crime? By being burned to death at the stake in front of a Texarkana mob of numbering more than "probably 6,000" people. As the newspaper reported, Coy, described as a "negro brute," allegedly "outraged" Julia Jewell, the wife of Henry Jewell and "a respectable woman," at her home. In fact, the reporter takes great pains to paint the Jewell family as the very picture of innocence and domestic bliss; in a section of the article headlined, "History of the Crime," the reporter relays this information: "When Mr. Jewell left his home on Saturday last after dinner to come to town for the transaction of some necessary business, he left his young wife, with her babe in her arms, in the best of health and spirits, little dreaming when he kissed her good-bye the terrible fate that awaited her during his absence." Such a picture of the couple is all the more perverse, perhaps deliberately so, if the alternative narrative of events, as will be discussed below, was true.

The "terrible fate" that befell Julia Jewell that Saturday, February 13, was the arrival of a Black man who "gave his name as Davis, and said he had some hogs to sell to Mr. Jewell." After conversing with this person, Jewell then "concluded to visit a neighbor half a mile distant, and went out to lock the door, when the negro, who was in hiding, sprang from his place of concealment," and after a struggle, he "succeeded in accomplishing his diabolical purpose." The man, later identified as Ed Coy, "then dragged the fainting woman into the barn where he kept her for about an hour, assaulting her repeatedly," before leaving and disappearing into the woods. When Henry Jewell returned, "he lost no time in giving the alarm," and posses were soon scouring the country "in all directions." Two Black men "answering the general description given by Mrs. Jewell" were brought before her but pronounced innocent. Soon, word spread that Coy had been seen heading northward in the direction of Little River County. On Thursday, February 18, another Black man was arrested and, though pronounced innocent by Julia Jewell, acknowledged having recently been with Coy and even having swapped clothes with him. Local authorities telegraphed the city of Hot Springs for bloodhounds as they ramped up their efforts to locate Coy, who was finally discovered hiding at the house of Ed Givens, a Black man living on the farm of W. B. Scott five miles from Texarkana.

The posse arrived and captured Coy, escorting him to Texarkana under the gaze of fifty mounted guards on the morning of Saturday, February 20, one week after the alleged crime. The leaders of the posse reportedly consulted on the best way to execute Coy and settled on hanging, but when they arrived at the intended place of execution, the mob began to shout, "Burn him!" And as the *Gazette* reported, "Some one at this juncture fired a Winchester and the excitement became indescribable. . . . [I]t was clearly to be seen that death by fire alone would alone [sic] appease the wrath of the surging multitude." After one "old citizen" urged the crowd to burn Coy outside of town "for the sake of their wives and children," the mob followed a "route to the suburbs" and, "when just over the Iron Mountain Railway track," found what was described as a "single stump about ten feet high, seasoned and strong," to which Coy was secured "with iron fastenings" and doused with kerosene.

The crowd, at this juncture, demanded the presence of Julia Jewell, the woman who had allegedly been raped by Coy. As Philip Dray notes:

This was a ritualized aspect of a Southern lynching. The woman who had been outraged was, when possible, asked to confront and identify her assailant and could, if she chose, participate in killing him, although in the actual bloodletting she was usually represented by a father, brother, husband, or other male relative, whose honor was deemed also to have been besmirched. That she be made to face her attacker and identify him was a somewhat curious tradition, considering that one of the frequent rationales for lynchings was that summary execution of rapists spared humiliated women the distress of having to answer questions in open court about the outrage they'd suffered.[42]

According to the *Gazette*, Jewell was an active participant in the death of Coy: "Pale, but determined, and supported on either side by a male relative, the little woman walked to the place of execution, where her assailent [*sic*] stood pinioned, struck a parlor match and applied it to the wretch in two places and stepped away. In a few moments the doomed darkey was a sheet of flame, writing and groaning in his horrible agony. Death resulted in about ten minutes." The account ends with the statement that the burning was "justified by a large majority of the people of this section, on the ground that a desperate disease requires a heroic remedy, and that hanging was not as great a punishment as the wretch deserved."[43]

Despite one prominent individual, Julia Jewell, being named in reports as having literally struck the match that killed Ed Coy, "the verdict of the Coroner's Jury was that Ed Coy came to his death by being burned at the stake by unknown parties." This topos of Southern lynching reports can perhaps be explained by the sacrificial ritual aspect of such mob violence, in which, the deed having been perpetrated collectively for the reconciliation of the group, "the responsibility for the death of the victim is shared by the group homogenously, so much so that no single member can be identified as an executioner," according to Palaver. "All are involved in a communal killing, without any single member committing murder."[44] Meanwhile, the town of Texarkana was reported to be "remarkably quiet; no excitement or demonstrations of any kind," although tourists were visiting the city to chip off pieces of the stump to which he was chained for souvenirs, "while all enterprising photographers are selling his pictures."[45] In fact, the following month, the *Gazette* reported, in a brief blurb on the first page, "the cedar stump to which Ed Coy was burned has been manufactured into cuff buttons."[46] As Palaver writes, "One finds numerous references in traditional folk culture to criminals who were sacralized after their execution. The remains of executed criminals (body parts, blood, etc.), as well as any arbitrary object (clothing, splinters from the gallows, the hangman's noose) with which they came into contact, were venerated as sacred relics."[47] Dray likewise observes that the many ritualistic aspects of lynching—"the use of fire, the sacredness of objects associated with the killing, the symbolic taking of trophies of the victim's remains, the sense of celebratory anticipation and then the lingering importance participants placed on such events—all suggest an anthropological basis for viewing lynching as a form of tribal sacrifice."[48]

Correspondents with both the *Arkansas Gazette* and the *Republic* of St. Louis, Missouri, managed to interview Ed Coy shortly before he was executed at the stake, and the condemned man insisted upon his innocence to both. Coy reported that the reason he fled the previous Saturday was "because he was told the Sheriff was after him for gambling," and that at one point, hiding out in a house in Texarkana, he considered turning himself in but "was told by the negroes that if he did so he would be lynched."[49] And subsequent investigations into the lynching of Coy would also assert his innocence. Later that year, the noted former Union soldier, writer, legislator, and civil rights activist Albion Winegar Tourgée wrote about the Coy case in the *Daily Inter Ocean* newspaper of Chicago in October 1892: "The woman who was paraded as a victim of violence was of bad character; her husband was a drunkard and a gambler. She was publicly reported and generally known to have been criminally intimate with Coy for more than a year previous. She was compelled by threats, if not by violence, to make the charge against the victim."[50] By the following year, Ida B. Wells was apparently citing more recent investigations by Tourgée that demonstrated that "Ed Coy had supported this woman (who was known to be a bad character) and her drunken husband for over a year previous to the burning."[51] (These characterizations of Jewell speak to Smångs's observation on the expansion of racial respectability even to the lower classes of whites in the postbellum years.) The counternarrative that Coy was in a consensual relationship with Julia Jewell was not only long lasting but also prevalent across the United States, with the Reverend D. A. Graham referencing Coy during a sermon he delivered in Indianapolis on the subject of Southern lynchings seven years later, saying of Julia Jewell that "relatives and husband of the woman who made the charge were fully cognizant of the fact that she was equally guilty with Coy. They compelled her to make the charge and then to set fire to her paramour."[52]

It is no accident, according to historian Amy Louise Wood, that "spectacle lynchings" of this kind, which featured ritualized violence in front of massive crowds, occurred in places like Texarkana, for such violence was closely related to the economic transformations underway in the South as a whole:

> Racial violence surged at the turn of the century, however, not because southern communities were cut off from modern institutions and customs but because they were undergoing an uncertain and troubled transformation into modern, urban societies. The devastation and uncertainties of the rural economy after the Civil War pushed increasing numbers of southerners, white and Black, off the farm, and as northern investment poured into the South, cities and towns grew in area and population. The most spectacular lynchings took place not in the countryside but in these newly urbanizing places, where mobs hanged their victims from telegraph and telephone poles and where streetcars and railroads brought crowds to witness the violence. Even the smallest towns were undergoing an urbanization process of sorts. They were experiencing changes that white citizens regularly celebrated as progressive while lamenting what they saw as the corrosive effects of these changes on the social order.[53]

Texarkana was one of these modernizing communities, a county seat that, situated in the southwestern corner of the state, served as a gateway to the ever-developing West, especially with the advent of those railroad tracks the mob had to cross to find the ideal place to lynch Coy. And it is no accident that African Americans in this era would be especially susceptible to lynching, for they remained sufficiently marginal to the community without ever being entirely outside it, being considered, in the words of sociologist Orlando Patterson, "a vast mass of domestic enemies, an army of masterless slaves" whose status represented a "collective loss of honor" for Southern whites.[54] No wonder, then, that allegations of rape would be sufficiently efficacious to motivate a lynching. Statistically, rape was not the most common motivation underlying a lynching; in 1890s Arkansas, nineteen lynchings were predicated upon sexual assault, while twenty-eight were based upon property crimes and fifty-five upon murder, according to one tabulation.[55] Or as Sommerville asserts, "the vitriolic clamor about black rape belied the extent to which black-on-white rape ostensibly precipitated lynchings."[56] In an era when even the acknowledged eloping of Black men and white women could draw the wrath of a mob, allegations of interracial rape would have been especially potent for white communities undergoing a crisis of identity and seeking to establish their boundaries of collective identity more firmly. As Smångs writes:

> Public lynchings did not simply affirm clearly or consensually defined collective racial identifications and solidarities among southern whites but directed racial group-formation processes by bringing them together in an active appreciation of the "true" nature of race relations, including the necessity of a cohesive white community standing united against the perceived black menace. The communalism, symbolism, and ritualism of public lynchings allowed whites, perpetrators and spectators alike, to enact and embody the core beliefs of extremist white supremacy as well as to attach themselves to each other, thereby transforming symbolic racial boundaries and categories into

> collective racial identifications and solidarities.
> ... Public lynchings were a collective ritual that
> not only revealed but also realized the white
> racial community in the emerging Jim Crow
> South.[57]

In short, lynching served exactly the purpose that Girard proposed for the scapegoat mechanism: unifying the community. As such, it functions as political violence, which, according to philosopher Paul Dumouchel, "is violence that structures and brings people together. It establishes groups. It unites and divides at the same time."[58] And such unification can only be achieved if the whole community takes part, as literary historian Trudier Harris notes:

> Acts of ritualized violence require group
> participation in order that the individuals
> involved may avoid feelings of guilt. The
> procedure can be compared to that used in
> firing squads where all squadsmen must fire at
> the victim and thereby be blamed and blameless,
> guilty and guiltless. The concept of law and order
> destroyed the offender, not the men pulling
> the triggers. In like manner, various concepts,
> not individuals, destroy black victims. Usually
> punished for disregarding some traditional
> taboo, the black men and women serve in their
> deaths to establish these practices as inviolable.[59]

Indeed, there is a dialectical relationship between "those who placed the rough noose around the neck or the flammable wood at the feet of the mob's victim" and those who encouraged or simply observed the actions of the active participants, according to Ashraf H. A. Rushdy, who thus describes the typical spectacle lynching as "a situation where the act of murder requires a mob to make it meaningful, and where a mob becomes the excuse people use to justify their action or their presence."[60] As rhetorician Megan Eatman observes, "Even if some white audience members were disgusted, their presence in the group contributed to the white supremacist spectacle." Moreover, this experience of "shared violence and a narrative of strength and victimhood" helped to erase distinctions, especially economic distinctions, among white Southerners and thus concealed "other possible understandings of what being a white Southerner could mean."[61] The collective participation means that no individual is responsible, which means that the victim was killed by no agent but, instead, met his death at the hands of a "concept." In other words, collective participation in this manner rendered the butchery on display another example of structural violence (see chapter 2).

In many ways, the scapegoating form of violence serves as the culmination of the other types of violence we have so far explored within the phenomenon of lynching. Lynching is group violence, perpetrated by a collectivity upon individuals who serve as representatives for another collectivity. The goal of lynching is fundamentally structural, to preserve the exploitable station of the target population. As the scapegoat must be marginal to the community rather than outside of it completely, lynching actually recognizes the humanity of its victim, for only a human victim can serve to settle the mimetic crisis at hand. Solving that crisis is the highest virtue, for it ensures the preservation of the community and facilities its return to "normal"—except that, no matter how many people they lynched, white society never quite seemed to return to normal.

CONCLUSION

*There must be something vile in us to make us
linger, age after age, in this insanitary spot.*

—Rebecca West, *Black Lamb and Grey Falcon*[1]

WE DO NOT CURRENTLY HUNT WITCHES. That is,
we do not, as a nation, have established legal institutions
whose responsibilities center upon investigations into
supernatural acts, with the aim of punishing those men
and women who perform such anti-miracles. Yes, we may
still engage in cultural practices that collectively punish
those whose ideology stands at variance with reigning
doctrine, or those whose practices have been taken to
represent, by some twisted metonymy, an affinity for
said outsider ideology. We may well seek scapegoats for
our personal setbacks, and we may still take a particular
delight in the downfall of independent women. Our
police officers may often act like the old witchfinders who
roamed the countryside and directed their fire against the
marginalized, and our criminal justice system may well
be permeated with beliefs and practices that echo the
notorious 1487 treatise on witchcraft, *Malleus Maleficarum*.
But here, in the United States, and now, in the twenty-first
century, we do not *literally* hunt witches.

However, the term *witch hunt* continues to be applied

metaphorically to various moral panics and mass hysterias in an attempt to equate them with the irrationality that we now locate in those olden witch hunts. When innocents are drawn into a spiral of accusations overseen by a monomaniacal figure of single-minded purpose who is blind to the destruction wrought by his attempts, as he sees them, to purify the population of heresy and disorder—then we feel comfortable calling this process a *witch hunt*. Arthur Miller's 1953 play *The Crucible*, which dramatizes the Salem Witch Trials, helped to cement the metaphorical application of the term, given that the play was explicitly intended as a criticism of Senator Joseph McCarthy and the Second Red Scare. However, powerful terms can be double-edged swords. The same word or idea employed to draw attention to a fundamental injustice can also be wielded to slander the mechanisms of justice itself. Thus did former president Donald Trump, who openly admitted his criminal activities, describe congressional hearings into those activities as a *witch hunt*, and although such a comparison constitutes an absolute obscenity to anyone with the most meager historical consciousness, the viability of the analogy, for Trump's explicit political purposes, rested upon the willingness of his followers to interpret events within that particular frame.

This president also described these congressional hearings as a *lynching*, which raises a somewhat different set of questions, since this application of the term was obviously metaphorical.[2] We do not currently have literal witch hunts, but do we continue to have, in the United States, literal lynchings? For scholars such as Christopher Waldrep and Ashraf H. A. Rushdy, the word *lynching* constitutes more a discourse than a discrete phenomenon, and that discourse can be and has been shaped—warped—by agents who, through malice or ignorance or other motivations, end up robbing said term of its power through a broader application than was originally intended. The latest example is, of course, the aforementioned president undergoing the process of his first impeachment, employing that terminology in order to wrap himself in martyr's robes and designate any act against him some species of persecution. Is there any feasible way in which an impeachment resembles a lynching?

In my introduction, I defined lynching as

- a scapegoating form of lethal violence;
- performed by one group of human beings against another group of human beings (or an individual representing said group) assigned lower moral status;
- for purposes regarded as virtuous by its perpetrators, such as punishment and regulation;
- with the effect of maintaining the very structural inequalities that delineate group boundaries and their respective moral statuses.

The problem with examining lynching solely as discourse is that bad actors can shape the discourse by appropriating its terminology. Thus, the employment of a discrete definition centered on the types of violence actually present in the behavior of lynching gives us more solid ground upon which to offer a critique of such appropriations. And as I hope would be obvious by the definition used here, the impeachment of a president on criminal allegations in no way resembles a lynching. In fact, the president's appropriation of the term *lynching* is what novelist and activist Sarah Schulman has called the "practice of overstating harm." Such overstatements result from a "conflation of Conflict with Abuse" and fundamentally serve "as a justification for cruelty": "namely, false accusations of harm are used to avoid an acknowledgment of complicity in creating conflict and instead escalate normative conflict to the level of crisis."[3] And false accusations of harm served as the basis for many a historical case of actual lynching, which better aligns Trump's behavior with the mob than with the victim hanging from a noose or burned to ash in a fire.

Trump was certainly overstating the harm of impeachment, but not all such overstatements, however, need necessarily result from bad-faith efforts. Instead, they may stem from a desire to latch on to specific language in order to draw attention to a historical or enduring injustice. For example, many scholars of genocide have criticized similar overstatements of harm and the threat they pose to maintaining precise and legally actionable terminology. Legal scholar Payam Akhavan, for one, has lamented the "unfounded efforts to appropriate genocide and the historical imagery of the Holocaust" as fostering a "banalization of suffering" or representing "a political culture of recognition in which ownership of anguish is not merely a means of working through trauma . . . but also a means of achieving a form of celebrity."[4]

But Trump's appropriation of the term *lynching* could, arguably and ironically—if coincidentally—have its roots in the rhetoric and imagery adopted by twentieth-century anti-lynching activists who compared this form of violence to the crucifixion of Christ. For example, the December 1911 issue of *The Crisis* featured a lynching photograph displayed alongside a cross and the mournful face of Jesus and titled *Jesus Christ in Georgia*.[5] Likewise did the Harlem Renaissance poet Countee Cullen write, in his 1922 poem

"Christ Recrucified," "But lest the sameness of the cross should tire / They kill him now with famished tongues of fire, / And while he burns, good men, and women, too / Shout, battling for his black and brittle bones."[6] For Black Christians, the comparison seemed particularly apt; false charges of criminal misdeed, an execution demanded by the mob, a long and tortuous death—not all of these were present at every lynching, but they were common enough to facilitate the analogy. Too, there was rhetorical power in appropriating the identity of Christ for the victim of lynching, given that Southern whites were typically very public about their religiosity, and so the comparison automatically entailed an accusation of hypocrisy, charging these mobs with crucifying Christ all over again. Here, the innocence of Christ is the cornerstone. Comparing various scapegoat myths with that of the crucifixion narrative presented in the canonical Gospels, René Girard writes, "In biblical texts, victims are innocent and collective violence is to blame. In myths, the victims are to blame and communities are always innocent."[7] He elaborates further:

> Jesus is presented to us as the innocent victim of a group in crisis, which, for a time at any rate, is united against him. All the subgroups and indeed all the individuals who are concerned with the life and trial of Jesus end up by giving their explicit or implicit assent to his death: the crowd in Jerusalem, the Jewish religious authorities, and Roman political authorities, and even the disciples, since those who do not betray or deny Jesus actively take flight or remain passive.[8]

And modern Black thinkers in liberation theology have continued to draw parallels between the crucifixion and the practice of American lynching. For example, theologian

James H. Cone writes at the beginning of his 2011 book, *The Cross and the Lynching Tree*, "Until we can see the cross and the lynching tree together, until we can identify Christ with a 'recrucified' black body hanging from a lynching tree, there can be no genuine understanding of Christian identity in America, and no deliverance from the brutal legacy of slavery and white supremacy."[9]

In other words, more than a century of rhetorical battle against the practice has transformed *lynching* from something deserved of a criminal, especially a prototypical "Black beast," into a form of violence directed against the innocent. Novelist James Carroll has questioned the "ancient Christian impulse to associate extreme evil with the fate of Jesus, precisely as a way of refusing to be defeated by that evil." "At the Golgotha of the crucifixion," he writes, "death became the necessary mode of transcendence, first for Jesus and then, as Christians believe, for all." The application of the name "Golgotha" to such events as the Holocaust, however, raises an important question for Carroll: "Can mechanized mass murder be a mode of transcendence? . . . If Auschwitz must stand for Jews as the abyss in which meaning itself died, what happens when Auschwitz becomes the sanctuary of someone else's recovered piety?"[10] Indeed, while Cone and others may insist upon the necessity of understanding the specific historical context that produced lynching, the comparison of racial violence to an alleged event that is theologically imagined to transcend all human divisions, including race—moreover, an event that now lies at a two-thousand-year remove and thus constitutes myth more than it does history—may well serve to abstract and universalize lynching, rendering it another drama of unwarranted persecution, another example of good versus evil, stripped of the specificities of race, class, geography, and more.

Moreover, the theological emphasis upon the absolute innocence of Christ does not equate to the absolute guilt of lynching victims. Not that all or even most were likely complicit in the crimes of which they were accused—rather, that their guilt was socially constructed, given that it was inherent in their racial identity. And it was absolute.

So we return to the question: Are there manifestations of violence today that can be called lynchings? Or perhaps this question would better be phrased: Are there manifestations of violence in our present time that correlate to the practice of lynching? According to sociologist Jonathan Markowitz, "Lynching was always intended as a metaphor for, or a way to understand, race relations. While there were many different types of lynchings, lynch mobs typically worked to ensure that black audiences were aware of the strength of white supremacy and the costs of violating the boundaries of the racial order; at the same time, they wanted to reinforce images of white men as chivalrous protectors of white women."[11] As we have seen, the perpetrators of lynching, and their defenders in government and media, were typically open in their expressions about the utility and necessity of lynching to protect the racial order. By contrast, those who perpetrate and/or defend violence for the same motivation now are regarded as exhibiting the psychological condition of hate, a condition that is explicitly individualized, and their crimes are thus labeled hate crimes rather than lynchings. As sociologist Chris Gilligan points out, "The very idea of *hate* crime focuses attention on the state of mind of the offender."[12] He goes on to observe:

> The idea that racism was a psychological problem located in the minds of racists, rather than a product of the organisation of society,

was facilitated by the post-Second World War rise of the psychology industry in universities, in human resource management, in counterculture awareness-raising and self-actualisation programmes, and in crime-fighting. The resort to the law as a means of redress was an indication of the receding of the emancipatory dynamic of the Civil Rights era and the rise of a reformist belief in the state as an instrument for tackling racisms.[13]

This particular approach to matters of racism narrows the horizon of feasible action a society might undertake to address the problem. As scholars Christopher Kyriakides and Rodolfo D. Torres argue, the psychological turn, in essence, places any pursuit of equality "beyond human hands. The criminalization of dangerous emotion does not locate oppression within the social structure, the institutions of 'White Power,' nor does it admit to the contradiction between universal rights and the inability of the capitalist system to deliver those rights."[14] But the identification of racism and its attendant violence as a psychological problem is perhaps not as new as Gilligan and others might believe, for it correlates to some of the strategies employed to oppose the practice of lynching, what rhetorician Ersula J. Ore calls the "rhetoric of shame and blame" applied by anti-lynching activists, especially the Association of Southern Women for the Prevention of Lynching; thus it is perhaps no accident that such rhetoric also correlated to "the advent of a discourse characterized by a narrower definition of lynching, which proponents used to deny the continued practice of lynching during the 1940s onward."[15] At the time, it was no doubt regarded as a worthwhile strategy—to identify the mob with psychological derangement, and thus make lynching seem a lower-class affair (when, in reality, it was typically the opposite) as a means of breaking white solidarity and thus motivating boosters and businessmen to take a stance against such violence. And then, both activists and those boosters were likewise motivated to turn a blind eye toward the evolution of lynching into the discrete assassinations that occurred in the dead of night and haunted the South during the civil rights era, into the legitimized violence of law enforcement against racialized others, into the individual practice of armed self-defense against those who appear out of place. And if some act of violence threatens to recall the form and spirit of lynching, it can be dubbed a hate crime and its perpetrator(s) sufficiently pathologized so as to protect the state and broader society from being implicated in its performance.

Thus does the equation of lynching with any present-day event stoke significant controversy, for in our modern era, we do not have lynchings—we have hate crimes. We do not have communal celebrations of butchery and blood defended by leading voices of the era—we have isolated individuals, psychologically askew, who perpetrate murders for reasons of some personal, pathological motivation. And, as a consequence of this development, we do not have any unified opposition to the practice of lynching, however it might be manifest, but, instead, an array of disparate interests attempting to tackle issues of police violence, hate crimes, economic inequality, and political disfranchisement, as if these were separate matters and not simply varied manifestations of the same underlying structure. What Ashraf H. A. Rushdy calls the *end-of-lynching discourse* that arose in the 1930s and 1940s "has conflated the end of lynching with the onset of a racially tolerant modernity. And what is lost as a result of that discourse is the opportunity for more subtle analyses of what racial conditions were like then and are like now."[16] American society may not currently exhibit the form of lynching, but the function remains present in other manifestations of violence, both subjective and objective, both personal and structural. Ore sees at the center of lynching a rhetoric of citizenship and belonging that perpetually marks the Black body as the outsider, and it is this rhetorical core that allows us to link such events as the lynching of Emmett Till with the murder of Trayvon Martin by self-appointed "neighborhood watchman" George Zimmerman. As she writes:

> There is only one tradition that describes the conscious choice to profile a black boy to death as chivalrous, only one tradition that posits the conscious eradication of black life as an unfortunate, but nonetheless ugly, consequence of supposed black delinquency, and only one tradition that uses racial terror as a means of policing the boundaries between America's white "us" and its black "them": that tradition—what Ida B. Wells referred to as America's "national crime"—is lynching.[17]

But it can be difficult for us to recognize this continuity, despite some obvious parallels, such as the various slanders thrown at the victim, the requirement of national attention to force local law enforcement to act, and the total exoneration of the killers to great fanfare in the more conservative press. The era of lynching, we are told again and again, has long since ended, and any evocation of that word, any application of it to modern "tragedies," is overstating the case (although presidential appropriation to describe a nonracialized act of nonviolence like impeachment is, according to the same voices, entirely permissible).

Scholars beyond the field of history have come to the conclusion that violence is "constitutive," that, as rhetorician Megan Eatman writes, it "shapes the identities of victims and participants. Violence clarifies the division of 'us' and 'them.' We are just and strong, they are dangerous and deviant. Violence is thus not an interaction between discrete individuals, but a process that creates both subjects."[18] The events covered in this book, the indisputable lynchings of the past, are part of a broader "rhetorical ecology produced by practices of direct, structural, and cultural violence," an ecology that, in ways mirroring the reality of a biological ecosystem, "is hospitable to only certain identities and practices."[19] And it is this metaphor of an "ecology of violence" that allows us to draw more firm lines between the atrocities of the past and the policies of the present. After all, biological ecosystems do not exist in a state of homeostasis. They evolve throughout time as the conditions that created and maintain them change and as the organisms contained within themselves undergo evolution. But we can, with careful work, see similar creatures occupying similar roles within these ecosystems throughout time. It is not that the modern vigilantes like Zimmerman are necessarily directly descended from the lynchers of yore. However, with the slow diminishment of classical lynching, there was an ecological niche that went unoccupied—specifically, a niche for the informal and violent enforcement of white supremacy and the regulation of Black bodies. People like Zimmerman now occupy that ecological niche.

With this book, therefore, I hope that I have sufficiently

strengthened the case for recognizing a continuity of lynching across the years by explicating the five types of violence that, to me, seem to lie at the core of the practice. Recognizing how lynching specifically encompassed group, structural, humanistic, virtuous, and scapegoating forms of violence should help us track its evolution, for any form of violence that exhibits these same qualities may, arguably, be compared with lynching, and we should not hesitate to apply the term and employ the full force of its rhetorical power. Using the right label can allow us to connect meaningfully with the past and recognize that the projects of previous generations of activists have not, in fact, been completed, but wait upon those now living to bring them to fruition. The end of lynching, unfortunately, lies before us still.

NOTES

INTRODUCTION

1. "How Can We Win," David Jones Media, video, 6:46, June 1, 2020, https://www.youtube.com/watch?v=sb9_qGOa9Go.

2. The terms *nightriding* and *whitecapping* were used interchangeably at the time to describe vigilante violence, often performed under cover of darkness or while disguised, specifically designed to intimidate an individual or group of people. Such violence could be racialized, as when poor whites organized to drive African Americans away from jobs or off their land, but such acts of intimidation were, just as often, perpetrated by whites against other whites, as when farmers banded together to prevent others from selling their cotton until the price had reached a level agreeable for all. For information on how the state defined nightriding/whitecapping, see CALS Encyclopedia of Arkansas, s.v. "Act 112 of 1902" by Guy Lancaster, last modified August 9, 2019, https://encyclopediaofarkansas.net/entries/act-112-of-1909-14368/.

3. James R. McGovern, *Anatomy of a Lynching: The Killing of Claude Neal* (Baton Rouge: Louisiana State University Press, 1982), 66.

4. Veena Das, *Life and Words: Violence and the Descent into the Ordinary* (Berkeley: University of California Press, 2007), 206.

5. The actual number of lynchings that occurred in Arkansas can vary widely, from the low three hundreds to nearly five hundred, depending upon what events are included—that is, whether one considers only those events that occurred following Reconstruction; whether one includes the lynching of whites alongside that of African Americans; and whether one includes mass-casualty events like the Elaine Massacre of 1919. For a survey of the disparities in these counts, see Guy Lancaster, "Introduction," in *Bullets and Fire: Lynching and Authority in Arkansas, 1840–1950*

(Fayetteville: University of Arkansas Press, 2018), 4–5. In addition, the online Encyclopedia of Arkansas maintains a chart of lynchings, updated regularly as new information arises; see CALS Encyclopedia of Arkansas, s.v. "Lynching," by Brent E. Riffel, last modified December 21, 2020, https://encyclopediaofarkansas.net/entries/lynching-346/.

CHAPTER 1

1. Vincent Vinikas, "Thirteen Dead at Saint Charles: Arkansas's Most Lethal Lynching and the Abrogation of Equal Protection," in *Bullets and Fire: Lynching and Authority in Arkansas, 1840–1950*, ed. Guy Lancaster (Fayetteville: University of Arkansas Press, 2018), 104.

2. "Five Negroes Shot to Death by Mob," *Arkansas Gazette*, March 26, 1904, 1; "Eleven Negroes Victims of Mob," *Arkansas Gazette*, March 27, 1904, 1.

3. Vinikas, "Thirteen Dead at Saint Charles," 125.

4. Vinikas, 105.

5. Vinikas, 110.

6. Christopher Waldrep, *The Many Faces of Judge Lynch: Extralegal Violence and Punishment in America* (New York: Palgrave Macmillan, 2002), 182.

7. Ashraf H. A. Rushdy, *American Lynching* (New Haven, CT: Yale University Press, 2012), 6–7.

8. James Elbert Cutler, *Lynch Law: An Investigation into the History of Lynching in the United States* (New York: Longmans, Green, & Co., 1905), 276.

9. Cited in Waldrep, *The Many Faces of Judge Lynch*, 2. After the conference, each of these rival organizations abandoned the definition because they found it incongruent with their own organizational goals.

10. W. Fitzhugh Brundage, *Lynching in the New South: Georgia and Virginia, 1880–1930* (Urbana: University of Illinois Press, 1993), 18.

11. Rushdy, *American Lynching*, 20.

12. James Hawdon and John Ryan, "Introduction: Working toward Understanding Group Violence," in *The Causes and Consequences of Group Violence: From Bullies to Terrorists*, ed. James Hawdon, John Ryan, and Marc Lucht (Lanham, MD: Lexington Books, 2014), x.

13. Paul Dumouchel, *The Barren Sacrifice: An Essay on Political*

Violence, trans. Mary Baker (East Lansing: Michigan State University Press, 2015), 41.

14. Gunnar Myrdal, *An American Dilemma: The Negro Problem and Modern Democracy* (New York: Harper & Brothers Publishers), 566.

15. Gilles Vandal, *Rethinking Southern Violence: Homicides in Post–Civil War Louisiana, 1866–1884* (Columbus: Ohio State University Press, 2000), 92.

16. Donald L. Horowitz, *The Deadly Ethnic Riot* (Berkeley: University of California Press, 2001), 1.

17. Horowitz, *Deadly Ethnic Riot*, 79, 89, 116–17.

18. Ann V. Collins, *All Hell Broke Loose: American Race Riots from the Progressive Era through World War II* (Santa Barbara, CA: Praeger, 2012), xvi.

19. Collins, 5.

20. Philip G. Dwyer and Lyndall Ryan, "The Massacre and History," in *Theatres of Violence: Massacre, Mass Killing and Atrocity throughout History*, ed. Philip G. Dwyer and Lyndall Ryan (New York: Berghahn Books, 2012), xv.

21. Dwyer and Ryan, xv.

22. Dwyer and Ryan, xvii.

23. Alex J. Bellamy, *Massacres and Morality: Mass Atrocities in an Age of Civilian Immunity* (New York: Oxford University Press, 2012), 28.

24. Larry May, *Genocide: A Normative Account* (New York: Cambridge University Press, 2010), 30–32.

25. May, 47.

26. Berel Lang, *Genocide: Act as Idea* (Philadelphia: University of Pennsylvania Press, 2017), 75–76.

27. Lang, 79.

28. Patrick Colm Hogan, *Understanding Nationalism: On Narrative, Cognitive Science, and Identity* (Columbus: The Ohio State University Press, 2009), 39

29. Hogan, 43.

30. Ariela J. Gross, *What Blood Won't Tell: A History of Race on Trial in America* (Cambridge, MA: Harvard University Press, 2008), 10.

31. Gross, 36.

32. Paul C. Taylor, *Race: A Philosophical Introduction*, 2nd ed. (Malden, MA: Polity Press, 2013), 89–90.

33. David Livingstone Smith, *On Inhumanity: Dehumanization*

and *How to Resist It* (New York: Oxford University Press, 2020), 102.

34. Claudia Card, *Confronting Evils: Terrorism, Torture, Genocide* (New York: Cambridge University Press, 2010), 79.

35. James Hawdon, "Group Violence Revisited: Common Themes across Types of Group Violence," in *The Causes and Consequences of Group Violence: From Bullies to Terrorists*, ed. James Hawdon, John Ryan, and Marc Lucht (Lanham, MD: Lexington Books, 2014), 248.

36. Wolfgang Palaver, *René Girard's Mimetic Theory*, trans. Gabriel Borrud (East Lansing: Michigan State University Press, 2013), 66.

37. Patrick Wolfe, *Traces of History: Elementary Structures of Race* (New York: Verso, 2016), 18.

38. Jan Voogd, *Race Riots and Resistance: The Red Summer of 1919* (New York: Peter Lang, 2008), 19.

39. Arne Johan Vetlesen, *Evil and Human Agency: Understanding Collective Evildoing* (New York: Cambridge University Press, 2005), 186.

40. Berel Lang, *Act and Idea in the Nazi Genocide* (Syracuse, NY: Syracuse University Press, 2003), 19.

41. Ziya Us Salam, *Lynch Files: The Forgotten Saga of Victims of Hate Crimes* (New Delhi: SAGE Publications India, 2019), 4.

42. "A Ghastly Find," *Arkansas Gazette*, March 12, 1894, 1.

43. "Mob Kills Negro: Riot Threatened," *Arkansas Gazette*, December 21, 1909, 1.

44. "Mob Kills Negro."

45. "Mob Kills Negro."

46. "Kill Negro, Burn House and Church," *Arkansas Gazette*, January 17, 1916, 8; "Prosecutor May Go to Buckville," *Hot Springs New Era*, January 18, 1916, 1.

47. *Lynching in America: Confronting the Legacy of Racial Terror*, 3rd ed. (Montgomery, AL: Equal Justice Initiative, 2017), 3, https://eji.org/reports/lynching-in-america/.

48. *Lynching in America*, 38.

49. *Lynching in America*, 39.

50. Andrew Strathern and Pamela J. Stewart, "Introduction: Terror, the Imagination, and Cosmology," in *Terror and Violence: Imagination and the Unimaginable*, ed. Andrew Strathern, Pamela J. Stewart, and Neil L. Whitehead (Ann Arbor, MI: Pluto Press, 2006), 7.

51. This is an analogy I first employed in my chapter, "'... or Suffer

the Consequences of Staying': Terror and Racial Cleansing in Arkansas," in *Historicizing Fear: Ignorance, Vilification, and Othering*, ed. Travis D. Boyce and Winsome M. Chunnu (Louisville: University Press of Colorado, 2019), 88–102.

52. Strathern and Stewart, "Introduction," 9.

53. Veena Das, *Life and Words: Violence and the Descent into the Ordinary* (Berkeley: University of California Press, 2007), 9.

54. Card, *Confronting Evils*, 166.

55. Vinikas, "Thirteen Dead at Saint Charles," 127.

56. Thomas C. Wright, *State Terrorism in Latin America: Chile, Argentina, and International Human Rights* (Lanham, MD: Rowman and Littlefield, 2007), 10.

57. Card, *Confronting Evils*, 167.

58. Stephanie Harp, "Stories of a Lynching: Accounts of John Carter, 1927," in *Bullets and Fire: Lynching and Authority in Arkansas, 1840–1950*, ed. Guy Lancaster (Fayetteville: University of Arkansas Press, 2018), 197.

59. Harp, 201.

60. Harp, 204.

61. Harp, 205.

62. Santana Khanikar, *State, Violence, and Legitimacy in India* (New Delhi: Oxford University Press, 2019), 101.

63. Vetlesen, *Evil and Human Agency*, 158.

64. See Shanika Smith, "The Success and Decline of Little Rock's West Ninth Street." *Pulaski County Historical Review* 67 (Summer 2019): 41–50.

65. "DeWitt Mob Takes Negro from Jail and Lynches Him," *Arkansas Democrat*, October 9, 1916, 8; "Negro Is Lynched by Mob at DeWitt," *Arkansas Gazette*, October 10, 1916, 1.

66. "In Arkansas County," *Arkansas Gazette*, March 29, 1904, 4.

CHAPTER 2

1. Simone de Beauvoir, *The Ethics of Ambiguity*, trans. Bernard Frechtman (New York: Citadel Press, 1948), 119.

2. *Public and Private Acts and Joint and Concurrent Resolutions and Memorials of the General Assembly of the State of Arkansas, 1909* (Little Rock: Secretary of State, 1909), 778–80.

3. "Two-Day Bill Passed the Senate," *Arkansas Gazette*, January 26, 1909, 3; "News and Notes of the Legislature," *Arkansas Gazette*, February 11, 1909, 3.

4. "To Prevent Lynchings," *Arkansas Gazette*, February 16, 1909, 5.

5. "Pickett Negroes Here," *Arkansas Gazette*, January 23, 1909, 2; "Charged with Murder," *Arkansas Gazette*, March 29, 1909, 1; "Soldiers Guard Jail at El Dorado," *Arkansas Gazette*, March 30, 1909, 1; "Negroes Reported Lynched," *Arkansas Gazette*, March 20, 1909, 1; "21 Years Given Pickett Negroes," *Arkansas Gazette*, April 2, 1909, 1.

6. "News and Notes of the Legislature," *Arkansas Gazette*, April 8, 1909, 12; "In the House, Wednesday, May 12, 1909," *Arkansas Gazette*, May 13, 1909, 3.

7. "Negro Assailant Escapes Lynching," *Arkansas Gazette*, May 12, 1909, 2; "Will Try Abe Green Tuesday," *Arkansas Gazette*, May 30, 1909, 1; "Green Sentenced to Die," *Arkansas Gazette*, June 6, 1909, 2.

8. "May Stop a Hanging," *Arkansas Gazette*, June 27, 1909, 5; "Abe Green to Hang," *Arkansas Gazette*, July 5, 1909, 3; "Proceedings in Supreme Court," *Arkansas Gazette*, July 6, 1909, 3; "Abe Green Will Not Be Hanged," *Arkansas Democrat*, October 11, 1909, 10.

9. "Drastic Bill by Senator Oldham," *Arkansas Gazette*, January 23, 1907, 2; "Suppression of Mob Violence," *Arkansas Gazette*, January 27, 1907, 16. Senator Robb died the following month on February 10 from bronchial pneumonia at the age of forty-five, and the *Gazette* report on his death devoted a great deal of space to his opposition to the Oldham bill. See "State Senator Howard Robb Dead," *Arkansas Gazette*, February 11, 1907, 1–2.

10. "Many Measures Are Discussed," *Arkansas Gazette*, February 10, 1907, 7.

11. "Oldham Anti-Lynching Bill Is Defeated by the House," *Arkansas Gazette*, April 28, 1907, 3.

12. "Endorses Oldham Bill," *Arkansas Gazette*, February 7, 1907, 2.

13. Ersula J. Ore, *Lynching: Violence, Rhetoric, and American Identity* (Jackson: University of Mississippi Press, 2019), 50.

14. Michael J. Pfeifer, *The Roots of Rough Justice: Origins of American Lynching* (Urbana: University of Illinois Press, 2011), 89.

15. Patrick Colm Hogan, *Understanding Nationalism: On Narrative, Cognitive Science, and Identity* (Columbus: The Ohio State University Press, 2009), 172–73.

16. Sonja Schillings, *Enemies of All Humankind: Fictions of*

Legitimate Violence (Hanover, NH: Dartmouth College Press, 2017), 2.

17. "Negro Admits Attack on Girl," *Pine Bluff Daily Graphic*, May 23, 1909, 1; "Pine Bluff Girl Is Choked by Negro," *Arkansas Gazette*, May 24, 1909, 2. An April report from Pine Bluff mentions one Lovett Davis who was an escaped Louisiana convict captured in Pine Bluff, but no reports on the arrest of Davis in May and his subsequent lynching mention him being from Louisiana. A later report in the *Arkansas Gazette* said that David hailed from Atlanta, Georgia. See "Louisiana Convict Captured Here," *Pine Bluff Daily Graphic*, April 20, 1909, 1; "Judge Grace Goes after Lynchers," *Arkansas Gazette*, May 27, 1909, 1.

18. "Mob at Pine Bluff Lynches a Negro," *Arkansas Gazette*, May 25, 1909, 1–2.

19. "Grand Jury Inquiries," *Arkansas Democrat*, May 26, 1909, 4; "Judge Grace to Probe Lynching," *Arkansas Gazette*, May 26, 1909, 1; "Judge Grace Goes after Lynchers," *Arkansas Gazette*, May 27, 1909, 1; "Making a Thorough Inquiry in Lynching," *Arkansas Democrat*, May 28, 1909, 12; "Grand Jury Is Probing Lynching," *Arkansas Gazette*, May 28, 1909, 2.

20. "Judge Scores Lynchers," *Batesville Guard*, June 4, 1909, 2

21. "Killing of a Dog Leads to Lynching." *Arkansas Gazette*, May 31, 1909, 1; "Murderer's Brother Is Lynched." *Broad Ax* (Salt Lake City, Utah), June 5, 1909, 2.

22. "Judge Deplores Lynching of Negro," *Arkansas Gazette*, June 21, 1913, 1 (the *Gazette* names him "Cotnam," but "Cotham" is the proper spelling).

23. Guy Lancaster, *Racial Cleansing in Arkansas, 1883–1924: Politics, Land, Labor, and Criminality* (Lanham, MD: Lexington Books, 2014), 103–107.

24. Paul Dumouchel, *The Barren Sacrifice: An Essay on Political Violence*, trans. Mary Baker (East Lansing: Michigan State University Press, 2015), xii.

25. Slavoj Žižek, *Violence* (New York: Picador, 2008), 2.

26. James A. Tyner, *Violence in Capitalism: Devaluing Life in an Age of Responsibility* (Lincoln: University of Nebraska Press, 2016), 3, 4.

27. Johan Galtung, "Violence, Peace, and Peace Research," *Journal of Peace Research* 6, no. 3 (1969): 168.

28. Galtung, "Violence, Peace, and Peace Research," 171.

29. Claudia Card, *Confronting Evils: Terrorism, Torture, Genocide* (New York: Cambridge University Press, 2010), 168.

30. Mattias Smångs, *Doing Violence, Making Race: Lynching and White Racial Group Formation in the U.S. South, 1882–1930* (New York: Routledge, 2017), 103.

31. Chris M. Branam, "Another Look at Disfranchisement in Arkansas, 1888–1894," *Arkansas Historical Quarterly* 69 (Autumn 2010): 245–62; Randy Finley, "A Lynching State: Arkansas in the 1890s," in *Bullets and Fire: Lynching and Authority in Arkansas, 1840–1950*, ed. Guy Lancaster (Fayetteville: University of Arkansas Press, 2018), 61–85.

32. John William Graves, *Town and Country: Race Relations in an Urban-Rural Context, Arkansas, 1865–1905* (Fayetteville: University of Arkansas Press, 1990), 86.

33. William Pickens, *Bursting Bonds* (Boston: 1923), 25–26.

34. Graves, *Town and Country*, 150–63, 219–25.

35. Akhil Gupta, "On Structural Violence," in *Violence Studies*, ed. Kalpana Kannabiran (New Delhi: Oxford University Press, 2016), 350.

36. "Drunken Mob Makes an Attack on a Negro Normal School in Arkansas." *Arizona Republican*, June 30, 1897, 8; "General News." *Nebraska Advertiser*, September 24, 1897, 2.

37. Robert Thomas Kerlin, *The Voice of the Negro 1919* (New York: E. P. Dutton, 1920), 101–102, https://archive.org /details/voiceofnegro191900kerl.

38. Lancaster, *Racial Cleansing in Arkansas*, 45–82.

39. Calvin R. Ledbetter Jr., "Adoption of Initiative and Referendum in Arkansas: The Roles of George W. Donaghey and William Jennings Bryan," *Arkansas Historical Quarterly* 51 (1992): 199–223; Calvin R. Ledbetter Jr., *Carpenter from Conway: George Washington Donaghey as Governor of Arkansas 1909–1913* (Fayetteville: University of Arkansas Press, 1993); James F. Willis, "The Farmers' Schools of 1909: The Origins of Arkansas's Four Regional Universities," *Arkansas Historical Quarterly* 65 (Autumn 2006): 224–49.

40. Dumouchel, *Barren Sacrifice*, xiv.

41. "Posse Out after Harry Poe," *Arkansas Gazette*, January 27, 1910, 7.

42. "Negro Is Rushed to Little Rock," *Arkansas Gazette*, January 29, 1910, 2; "Negro Is Spirited Away," *Arkansas Gazette*, February 1, 1910, 1.

43. "Negro Must Hang at Hot Springs on April 1," *Arkansas Democrat*, March 2, 1910, 1; "Poe Appeal Was Mistake," *Sentinel-Record* (Hot Springs), March 3, 1910, 4; "Harry Poe's Execution Is Stayed by Appeal," *Arkansas Gazette*, March 25, 1910, 5. The *Gazette* has Poe being arrested and then "identified" on January 28, prior to his transfer from the county, but other sources have Poe committing his alleged crime on January 28 and being arrested two days later and positively identified on January 31; see "Harry Poe Forfeited His Life on Gallows Today for Rape," *Hot Springs Daily News*, September 2, 1910, 1. However, the actual chief of police docket records his arrest on January 26; see Garland County Records: Jail and Prison Records, 1884–1965: January 1, 1904, Docket of Police Judge— January 30, 1913, Police Judge Docket, microfilm, Arkansas State Archives, Little Rock.

44. "Decisions of Supreme Court," *Arkansas Gazette*, May 10, 1910, 10.

45. "Two Weeks Given for Brief in Poe Case," *Arkansas Gazette*, May 22, 1910, 5; "Decision of the Supreme Court," *Arkansas Gazette*, June 7, 1910, 9; "Negro Stoically Awaits His Death," *Arkansas Gazette*, July 21, 1910, 3.

46. "Plead for Harry Poe," *Sentinel-Record* (Hot Springs), June 16, 1910, 1.

47. "Will Send Militia to Attend Poe's Hanging," *Arkansas Gazette*, August 11, 1910, 9; "Asks Stay of Execution," *Arkansas Gazette*, August 31, 1910, 6.

48. Margaret Vandiver, *Lethal Punishment: Lynchings and Legal Executions in the South* (New Brunswick, NJ: Rutgers University Press, 2006), 13.

49. Matthew Rothberg, *The Implicated Subject: Beyond Victims and Perpetrators* (Stanford, CA: Stanford University Press, 2019), 1–2.

50. Card, *Confronting Evils*, 69.

51. Grif Stockley, *Black Boys Burning: The 1959 Fire at the Arkansas Negro Boys Industrial School* (Jackson: University Press of Mississippi, 2017), 83.

52. Quoted in Stockley, *Black Boys Burning*, 141.

53. "The Newport Lynching," *Arkansas Gazette*, January 3, 1905, 4.

54. "When Public Anger Breaks All Bonds," *Arkansas Gazette*, June 21, 1913, 6.

55. Mikkel Thorup, *An Intellectual History of Terror: War, Violence and the State* (New York: Routledge, 2010), 17.

56. Michelle Alexander, *The New Jim Crow: Mass Incarceration in the Age of Colorblindness* (New York: The New Press, 2010), 183–84.

57. Tanya Maria Golash-Boza, *Race and Racisms: A Critical Approach* (New York: Oxford University Press, 2015), 187

58. Tyner, *Violence in Capitalism*, 19.

59. Žižek, *Violence*, 9.

60. Tyner, *Violence in Capitalism*, 8.

61. Dumouchel, *The Barren Sacrifice*, 90.

62. Dumouchel, 91.

CHAPTER 3

1. Karlos Hill, *Beyond the Rope: The Impact of Lynching on Black Culture and Memory* (New York: Cambridge University Press, 2016), 51.

2. Hill, 40–49

3. Hill, 53.

4. Hill, 54.

5. "Negro Slayer Is Burned at Stake," *Arkansas Gazette*, January 27, 1921, 1.

6. Wolfgang Palaver, *René Girard's Mimetic Theory*, trans. Gabriel Borrud (East Lansing: Michigan State University Press, 2013), 288.

7. Hill, *Beyond the Rope*, 55.

8. Henry Kamen, *The Spanish Inquisition: A Historical Revision* (New Haven, CT: Yale University Press, 1997), 189.

9. Claudia Card, *Confronting Evils: Terrorism, Torture, Genocide* (New York: Cambridge University Press, 2010), 207.

10. Kjell Anderson, *Perpetrating Genocide: A Criminological Account* (New York: Routledge, 2018), 71.

11. Mikkel Thorup, *An Intellectual History of Terror: War, Violence and the State* (New York: Routledge, 2010), 15.

12. Eric D. Weitz, *A Century of Genocide: Utopias of Race and Nation* (Princeton, NJ: Princeton University Press, 2003), 239.

13. Jacqueline Dowd Hall, *Revolt against Chivalry: Jessie Daniel Ames and the Women's Campaign against Lynching* (New York: Columbia University Press, 1993), xxi.

14. Randy Finley, "A Lynching State: Arkansas in the 1890s," in *Bullets and Fire: Lynching and Authority in Arkansas, 1840–1950*,

ed. Guy Lancaster (Fayetteville: University of Arkansas Press, 2018), 70–71.

15. Fritz Breithaupt, *The Dark Sides of Empathy*, trans. Andrew B. B. Hamilton (Ithaca, NY: Cornell University Press, 2019), 84.

16. Kate Manne, *Down Girl: The Logic of Misogyny* (New York: Oxford University Press, 2018), 151.

17. Manne, 152.

18. Anderson, *Perpetrating Genocide*, 73.

19. David Livingstone Smith, *On Inhumanity: Dehumanization and How to Resist It* (New York: Oxford University Press, 2020), 91.

20. Berel Lang, *Act and Idea in the Nazi Genocide* (Syracuse, NY: Syracuse University Press, 2003), 22.

21. Lang, 21.

22. Breithaupt, *The Dark Sides of Empathy*, 1.

23. Breithaupt, 97.

24. Breithaupt, 99.

25. Breithaupt, 114.

26. Breithaupt, 177.

27. W. Fitzhugh Brundage, *Lynching in the New South: Georgia and Virginia, 1880–1930* (Urbana: University of Illinois Press, 1993), 39.

28. Breithaupt, *The Dark Sides of Empathy*, 181.

29. Robert J. Sternberg and Karin Sternberg, *The Nature of Hate* (New York: Oxford University Press, 2008), 51.

30. Sternberg and Sternberg, 54, 59.

31. Sternberg and Sternberg, 61.

32. Manne, *Down Girl*, 135.

33. "Assailant of Girl Lynched by Mob of 20," *Arkansas Democrat*, August 9, 1916, 1; "Miss Whitman's [*sic*] Assailant Pays Usual Penalty," *Pine Bluff Daily Graphic*, August 10, 1916, 1; "Negro Who Attacked Girl Is Lynched at Stuttgart," *Arkansas Gazette*, August 10, 1916, 12.

34. "Negro Is Lynched by Mob at DeWitt." *Arkansas Gazette*, October 10, 1916, 1.

35. "Mob Victim Was Extended Every Earned Courtesy," *Arkansas Democrat*, August 14, 1916, 1.

36. Manne, *Down Girl*, 134.

37. Manne, 157.

38. "Race Troubles near Star City Are Not Feared," *Pine Bluff Daily Graphic*, September 4, 1919, 1; "Lynching at Star City Followed by Reprisal Threats," *Arkansas Democrat*, September 3, 1919, 1.

39. Quoted in Robert Thomas Kerlin, *The Voice of the Negro 1919* (New York: E. P. Dutton, 1920), 103, https://archive.org /details/voiceofnegro191900kerl.

40. David F. Krugler, *1919, The Year of Racial Violence: How African Americans Fought Back* (New York: Cambridge University Press, 2015), 15–16.

41. Nan Elizabeth Woodruff, *American Congo: The African American Freedom Struggle in the Delta* (Cambridge, MA: Harvard University Press, 2003), 49.

42. Randy Finley, "Black Arkansans and World War One," *Arkansas Historical Quarterly* 49 (Autumn 1990): 261.

43. Woodruff, *American Congo*, 116.

44. Daniel C. Dennett, *Consciousness Explained* (Boston: Little, Brown, 1991), 76.

45. Andrew Whiten and Josef Perner, "Fundamental Issues in the Multidisciplinary Study of Mindreading," in *Natural Theories of Mind: Evolution, Development and Simulation of Everyday Mindreading*, ed. Andrew Whiten (Cambridge, MA: Basil Blackwell, 1991), 9.

46. Whiten and Perner, 10.

47. Manne, *Down Girl*, 147.

48. Kelly Houston Jones, "White Fear of Black Rebellion in Antebellum Arkansas, 1819–1865," in *The Elaine Massacre and Arkansas: A Century of Atrocity and Resistance, 1819–1919*, ed. Guy Lancaster (Little Rock: Butler Center Books, 2018), 17–39.

49. Michael Pierce, "The Mechanics of Little Rock: Free Labor Ideas in Antebellum Arkansas, 1845–1861," *Arkansas Historical Quarterly* 67 (Autumn 2008): 221.

50. Pierce, "The Mechanics of Little Rock," 233–35; Jones, "White Fear of Black Rebellion," 33–35.

51. Guy Lancaster, *Racial Cleansing in Arkansas, 1883–1924: Politics, Land, Labor, and Criminality* (Lanham, MD: Lexington Books, 2014), 45–74.

52. Manne, *Down Girl*, 148.

53. Manne, 168.

CHAPTER 4

1. "The Vengeance of the Mob," *Arkansas Gazette*, May 15, 1892, 4.
2. "D., S. THUD," *Arkansas Gazette*, May 14, 1892, 1. The title of the *Gazette's* article, "D., S. Thud" was an abbreviation for "dull, sickening thud," a term often used to describe the sound of someone being hanged.
3. "D., S. THUD," 1.
4. "He's Gone," *Arkansas Gazette*, May 14, 1892, 1.
5. Amy Louise Wood, *Lynching and Spectacle: Witnessing Racial Violence in America, 1890–1940* (Chapel Hill: University of North Carolina Press, 2009), 39.
6. Wood, 62.
7. "He's Gone," *Arkansas Gazette*, May 14, 1892, 1; "A Night's Work," *Arkansas Gazette*, May 15, 1892, 1, 3. For a more detailed account of the lynching of Henry James, see Guy Lancaster, "Before John Carter: Lynching and Mob Violence in Pulaski County, 1882–1906," in *Bullets and Fire: Lynching and Authority in Arkansas, 1840–1950*, ed. Guy Lancaster (Fayetteville: University of Arkansas Press, 2018), 170–78.
8. Alan Page Fiske and Tage Shakti Rai, *Virtuous Violence: Hurting and Killing to Create, Sustain, End, and Honor Social Relationships* (New York: Cambridge University Press, 2015), xxii.
9. Fiske and Rai, 2.
10. David Livingstone Smith, *On Inhumanity: Dehumanization and How to Resist It* (New York: Oxford University Press, 2020), 91.
11. René Girard, *The One by Whom Scandal Comes*, trans. M. B. DeBevoise (East Lansing: Michigan State University Press, 2014), 18.
12. Mikkel Thorup, *An Intellectual History of Terror: War, Violence and the State* (New York: Routledge, 2010), 21.
13. Fiske and Rai, *Virtuous Violence*, 7.
14. Fiske and Rai, 17.
15. Fiske and Rai, 18–21.
16. Fiske and Rai, 22–24.
17. Fiske and Rai, 37.
18. Fiske and Rai, 158, 159.
19. Kelly Houston Jones, "'Doubtless Guilty': Lynching and Slaves in Antebellum Arkansas," in *Bullets and Fire: Lynching*

and *Authority in Arkansas, 1840–1950*, ed. Guy Lancaster
(Fayetteville: University of Arkansas Press, 2018), 20.

20. *Biographical and Historical Memoirs of Southern Arkansas*
(Chicago: Goodspeed Publishing Co., 1890), 826.

21. Diary of George W. Lewis, June 4, 1865–December 31, 1865,
12th Michigan Infantry Regiment, Lloyd Miller Collection,
US Army Military History Institute, Carlisle Barracks,
Carlisle, Pennsylvania.

22. "Barbarous." *New York Herald*, April 17, 1873, 5.

23. "Mob Has Formed to Lynch Negro," *Arkansas Gazette*,
February 19, 1904, 1.

24. "Negro Murderer Burned at Stake," *Arkansas Gazette*,
February 20, 1904, 1–2.

25. "Negro Burned Alive by a Mob near El Dorado," *Arkansas
Gazette*, May 22, 1919, 1.

26. "Negro Who Slew Sheriff of Columbia County Is Burned
at Stake by Mob," *Arkansas Democrat*, November 11, 1919,
1; "Sheriff's Slayer Burned at Stake," *Arkansas Gazette*,
November 12, 1919, 9.

27. Wood, *Lynching and Spectacle*, 63–64.

28. Arne Johan Vetlesen, *Evil and Human Agency: Understanding
Collective Evildoing* (New York: Cambridge University Press,
2005), 185.

29. "Retribution." *Arkansas Gazette*, July 2, 1875, 4; "Lynch Law:
A Negro Hung near Russellville." *Arkansas Gazette*, June 29,
1875, 4.

30. "Lynchings," *Arkansas Gazette*, August 11, 1898, 4.

31. Richard Buckelew, "The Clarendon Lynching of 1898: The
Intersection of Race, Class, and Gender," in *Bullets and Fire:
Lynching and Authority in Arkansas, 1840–1950*, ed. Guy
Lancaster (Fayetteville: University of Arkansas Press, 2018), 100.

32. "The Lynching Mania," *Arkansas Gazette*, August 18, 1898, 4.

33. "As to Lynching," *Arkansas Gazette*, August 26, 1898, 4.

34. "Nathan Lacey Was Lynched Last Night," *Arkansas Democrat*,
October 17, 1911, 1; "Nathan Lacey Is Lynched by Mob,"
Arkansas Gazette, October 17, 1911, 1.

35. "Do Lynchings Pay?" *Arkansas Democrat*, October 18, 1911, 6.

36. "Some Questions," *The Appeal* (St. Paul, Minnesota), May 21,
1892, 2. *Lex talionis* is the Latin term for the law of retaliation,
or more commonly the "eye for an eye" form of justice.

CHAPTER 5

1. Aeschylus, *Oresteia*, trans. Peter Meineck (Indianapolis: Hackett Publishing Company, 1998), 101.

2. "Was Lynched for Eloping," *Arkansas Democrat*, July 7, 1905, 1.

3. "Dumas Scene of Quiet Lynching," *Arkansas Gazette*, July 7, 1905, 1. As Nancy Snell Griffith has noted, a number of reports concerning "private mob" lynchings depicted the mob as going about its work in a quiet and orderly fashion. See Nancy Snell Griffith, "'At the Hands of a Person or Persons Unknown': The Nature of Lynch Mobs in Arkansas," in *Bullets and Fire: Lynching and Authority in Arkansas, 1840–1950*, ed. Guy Lancaster (Fayetteville: University of Arkansas Press, 2018), 38–40.

4. "Brownstown [Sevier County]," *Arkansas Gazette*, October 4, 1887, 3.

5. "Negro Is Lynched in Chicot County," *Arkansas Gazette*, November 26, 1921, 1; "Note Written to White Girl Costs Young Negro His Life." *New York Tribune*, November 26, 1921, 6.

6. "Denounce Rape," *Arkansas Gazette*, August 20, 1899, 3.

7. Quoted in Fon Louise Gordon, *Caste and Class: The Black Experience in Arkansas, 1880–1920* (Athens: University of Georgia Press, 1995), 50.

8. Philip Dray, *At the Hands of Persons Unknown: The Lynching of Black America* (New York: Random House, 2002), 73.

9. Charles F. Robinson, "'Most Shamefully Common': Arkansas and Miscegenation," *Arkansas Historical Quarterly* 60 (Autumn 2001): 266.

10. Kelly Houston Jones, "'Doubtless Guilty': Lynching and Slaves in Antebellum Arkansas," in *Bullets and Fire: Lynching and Authority in Arkansas, 1840–1950*, ed. Guy Lancaster (Fayetteville: University of Arkansas Press, 2018), 33.

11. Dray, *At the Hands of Persons Unknown*, 29.

12. Diane Miller Somerville, *Rape and Race in the Nineteenth-Century South* (Chapel Hill: University of North Carolina Press, 2004), 24.

13. Robinson, "'Most Shamefully Common,'" 268.

14. Quoted in Paul C. Palmer, "Miscegenation as an Issue in the Arkansas Constitutional Convention of 1868," *Arkansas Historical Quarterly* 24 (Summer 1965): 102.

15. Joel Williamson, *The Crucible of Race: Black-White Relations in the American South since Emancipation* (New York: Oxford University Press, 1984), 43.

16. "Showed Their Hands," *Arkansas Gazette*, February 1, 1868, 2.

17. Palmer, "Miscegenation as an Issue," 119.

18. Robinson, "'Most Shamefully Common,'" 271–72.

19. Mattias Smångs, *Doing Violence, Making Race: Lynching and White Racial Group Formation in the U.S. South, 1882–1930* (New York: Routledge, 2017), 74.

20. Ashraf H. A. Rushdy, *American Lynching* (New Haven, CT: Yale University Press, 2012), 95.

21. Robinson, "'Most Shamefully Common,'" 275–76.

22. "A Whitecapper Killed," *Osceola Times*, May 5, 1894, 3.

23. Ida. B. Wells, "Lynch Law in All Its Phases," *Our Day*, May 1893; online at *BlackPast*, January 29, 2007, https://www.Blackpast.org/uncategorized/1893-ida-b-wells-lynch-law-all-its-phases/.

24. Wolfgang Palaver, *René Girard's Mimetic Theory*, trans. Gabriel Borrud (East Lansing: Michigan State University Press, 2013), 36.

25. Scott R. Garrels, "Imitation, Mirror Neurons, and Mimetic Desire: Convergence between the Mimetic Theory of René Girard and Empirical Research on Imitation," *Contagion: Journal of Violence, Mimesis, and Culture* 12–13 (2006): 64.

26. René Girard, *Violence and the Sacred*, trans, Patrick Gregory (Baltimore, MD: Johns Hopkins University Press, 1977), 146.

27. Girard, 145.

28. Girard, 146.

29. Kate Manne, *Down Girl: The Logic of Misogyny* (New York: Oxford University Press, 2018), 154.

30. Palaver, *René Girard's Mimetic Theory*, 38.

31. Palaver, 59.

32. Palaver, 61.

33. Michael E. Brown, "The Causes of Internal Conflict: An Overview," in *Nationalism and Ethnic Conflict*, rev. ed, ed. Michael E. Brown, Owen R. Coté Jr., Sean M. Lynn-Jones, and Steven E. Miller (Cambridge, MA: MIT Press, 2001), 11–12.

34. Donald G. Mathews, *At the Altar of Lynching: Burning Sam Hose in the American South* (New York: Cambridge University Press, 2018), 172.

35. René Girard, "Violence and Religion: Cause or Effect?" *The*

Hedgehog Review: Critical Reflections on Contemporary Culture 6 (Spring 2004): 8.

36. Arne Johan Vetlesen, *Evil and Human Agency: Understanding Collective Evildoing* (New York: Cambridge University Press, 2005), 182.

37. Girard, *Violence and the Sacred*, 270, 271.

38. Vetlesen, *Evil and Human Agency*, 183–84.

39. Vetlesen, 185.

40. Palaver, *René Girard's Mimetic Theory*, 152.

41. "At the Stake," *Arkansas Gazette*, February 21, 1912, 1.

42. Dray, *At the Hands of Persons Unknown*, 11–12.

43. "At the Stake," *Arkansas Gazette*, February 21, 1912, 1.

44. Palaver, *René Girard's Mimetic Theory*, 161.

45. "Coy's Carcass," *Arkansas Gazette*, February 23, 1892, 2.

46. "State News," *Arkansas Gazette*, March 11, 1892, 1.

47. Palaver, *René Girard's Mimetic Theory*, 288.

48. Dray, *At the Hands of Persons Unknown*, 79.

49. "At the Stake," *Arkansas Gazette*, February 21, 1912, 1.

50. Quoted in CALS Encyclopedia of Arkansas, s.v. "Ed Coy (Lynching of)," by Larry LeMasters, last modified July 2, 2016, https://encyclopediaofarkansas.net/entries/edward-coy-7035/.

51. Wells, "Lynch Law in All Its Phases" (punctuation modernized).

52. Rev. D. A. Graham, "Some Facts about Southern Lynchings," *Indianapolis Recorder*, June 10, 1899; online at *BlackPast*, January 29, 2007, http://www.Blackpast.org/?q=1899 -reverend-d-graham-some-facts-about-southern-lynchings.

53. Amy Louise Wood, *Lynching and Spectacle: Witnessing Racial Violence in America, 1890–1940* (Chapel Hill: University of North Carolina Press, 2009), 5–6.

54. Orlando Patterson, *Rituals of Blood: Consequences of Slavery in Two American Centuries* (Washington, DC: Civitas/ Counterpoint, 1998), 192.

55. Randy Finley, "A Lynching State: Arkansas in the 1890s," in *Bullets and Fire: Lynching and Authority in Arkansas, 1840–1950*, ed. Guy Lancaster (Fayetteville: University of Arkansas Press, 2018), 62.

56. Sommerville, *Rape and Race in the Nineteenth-Century South*, 200.

57. Smångs, *Doing Violence, Making Race*, 107, 109.

58. Paul Dumouchel, *The Barren Sacrifice: An Essay on Political*

Violence, trans. Mary Baker (East Lansing: Michigan State University Press, 2015), 91.

59. Trudier Harris, *Exorcising Blackness: Historical and Literary Lynching and Burning Rituals* (Bloomington: Indiana University Press, 1984), 12.

60. Ashraf H. A. Rushdy, *The End of American Lynching* (New Brunswick, NJ: Rutgers University Press, 2012), 27.

61. Megan Eatman, *Ecologies of Harm: Rhetorics of Violence in the United States* (Columbus: Ohio State University Press, 2020), 31, 32.

CONCLUSION

1. Rebecca West, *Black Lamb and Grey Falcon: A Journey through Yugoslavia* (New York: Viking, 1941), 830.

2. See Guy Lancaster, "Lynching and Impeachment: Some History for Donald Trump," *Arkansas Times*, October 22, 2019, https://arktimes.com/arkansas-blog/2019/10/22/lynching-and-impeachment-some-history-for-donald-trump.

3. Sarah Schulman, *Conflict Is Not Abuse: Overstating Harm, Community Responsibility, and the Duty of Repair* (Vancouver: Arsenal Pulp Press, 2018), 21, 23, 28.

4. Payam Akhavan, *Reducing Genocide to Law: Definition, Meaning, and the Ultimate Crime* (New York: Cambridge University Press, 2012), 131, 124. The terms *historical injustice* and *enduring injustice* are drawn from Jeff Spinner-Halev, *Enduring Injustice* (New York: Cambridge University Press, 2012).

5. Amy Louise Wood, *Lynching and Spectacle: Witnessing Racial Violence in America, 1890–1940* (Chapel Hill: University of North Carolina Press, 2009), 188–89.

6. Quoted from Anne P. Rice, ed., *Witnessing Lynching: American Writers Respond* (New Brunswick, NJ: Rutgers University Press, 2003), 220–22.

7. René Girard, *The One by Whom Scandal Comes*, trans. M. B. DeBevoise (East Lansing: Michigan State University Press, 2014), 35.

8. René Girard, *Things Hidden since the Foundation of the World*, trans. Stephen Bann and Michael Metteer (Stanford, CA: Stanford University Press, 1987), 167.

9. James H. Cone, *The Cross and the Lynching Tree* (Maryknoll, NY: Orbis Books, 2011), xv.

10. James Carroll, *Constantine's Sword: The Church and the Jews: A History* (Boston: Houghton Mifflin Company, 2001), 5.

11. Jonathan Markowitz, *Legacies of Lynching: Racial Violence and Memory* (Minneapolis: University of Minnesota Press, 2004), xvi.

12. Chris Gilligan, *Northern Ireland and the Crisis of Anti-Racism: Rethinking Racism and Sectarianism* (Manchester: Manchester University Press, 2017), 164.

13. Gilligan, 175.

14. Christopher Kyriakides and Rodolfo D. Torres, *Race Defaced: Paradigms of Pessimism, Politics of Possibility* (Stanford, CA: Stanford University Press, 2012), 156–57.

15. Ersula J. Ore, *Lynching: Violence, Rhetoric, and American Identity* (Jackson: University Press of Mississippi, 2019), 5–6.

16. Ashraf H. A. Rushdy, *The End of American Lynching* (New Brunswick, NJ: Rutgers University Press, 2012), 137.

17. Ore, *Lynching*, 10.

18. Megan Eatman, *Ecologies of Harm: Rhetorics of Violence in the United States* (Columbus: Ohio State University Press, 2020), 2.

19. Eatman, *Ecologies of Harm*, 9.

ACKNOWLEDGMENTS

As this book comes at the culmination of a long period of research into racial violence, stretching back to the days of my doctoral dissertation, I feel like I could simply copy and paste all the acknowledgments from my previous books and articles here and be done with it, in addition to thanking all the contributors to the edited volumes I have undertaken. However, there are certain individuals to whom I am personally indebted for this book. My friend and colleague Richard Buckelew, who wrote the first dissertation on lynching in Arkansas and so, in many ways, set this field in motion, read through various drafts of this manuscript and offered much good feedback, including the suggestion that, despite my hesitations, I attempt to take these ideas and fashion a concise definition of lynching from them. William A. Johnsen, one of the foremost scholars on René Girard, also read through the full text and offered significant encouragement for its publication. William H. Pruden III, a true scholar and gentleman, gave some wonderful feedback on some some early sections of this work, and the peer reviewers helped to save me from some of my more unfortunate compositional habits, as did copyeditor extraordinaire James Fraleigh. Grif Stockley has been a constant source of encouragement and inspiration who, despite his protestations otherwise, is a true historian in all respects, as well as a true humanitarian. Brian Mitchell and I covered much of the state during the various events of the year 2019, when the commemoration of the Elaine Massacre was in full swing, and so had a chance to discuss some of the ideas in this present volume.

Nancy Snell Griffith has written extensively about the many lynchings in the state for the online Encyclopedia of Arkansas, which certainly made putting this book together much easier, aside from just giving the citizens of this state and beyond the facts, as best as they can be determined, about our shared past. In addition, my new friends Kwami and Clarice Abdul-Bey have motivated me to think more deeply about lynching in their own work as co-conveners of the Arkansas Peace and Justice Memorial Movement, an organization dedicated to commemorating the state's history of racial violence with the aim of achieving reconciliation across boundaries of race, class, and belief. Alongside my day job, I have also now and then taught undergraduate and graduate classes as an adjunct professor, classes that touched upon some of the issues explored here, and I want to thank all of my students through the years for motivating me to think more deeply and precisely about the nature of racialized violence.

Every writer needs an editor who can share his or her vision and offer direction in exactly how to arrive at that promised land. Editor-in-chief David Scott Cunningham is just such a person, and it has been a treat to work with him and the staff of the University of Arkansas Press once again. I genuinely appreciate the commitment of the University of Arkansas Press, led by director Mike Bieker, to publish material that challenges how we look at our collective past. This was my first time working with the very capable managing editor Janet Foxman, and I look forward to doing so again. (Welcome to Arkansas, Janet!) Too, my good friend Stephanie Harp, a scholar of lynching in her own right and a damned fine proofreader, went through the text and found multiple small errors that I had missed, and I cannot thank her enough for helping me appear to be somewhat competent, as well as for her encouragement and enthusiasm.

Finally, this book would not exist without my wonderful wife, Anna, who insisted that I undertake my own project again—not another edited volume or coauthored work, but something I wrote alone. And she put up with me regularly descending into fits of absentmindedness, or running around in search of a notepad as the latest idea rose to the surface at inopportune moments, or occupying the kitchen table with various open-faced books because I had run out of space on my desk. I try my best not to fall into the stereotypes of typical scholars and writers, but when I do so fall, she is always there to catch me, and she always forgives me if dinner gets burned because I suddenly have to go look up a citation and then get lost again among my various books. And so I say to her, in those words that William Shakespeare put in the mouth of Henry Bolingbroke, that "all my treasury / Is yet but unfelt thanks, which more enrich'd / Shall be your love and labour's recompense."

INDEX

Abbott, Charles, 45
Abbott, F. M., 45
abduction from law
    enforcement, 42, 73, 110;
    from jail, 30, 52, 83–84,
    99–100, 117–18, 124
Act 100 of 1909, 62
Act 151 of 1859, 93
Act 258 of 1909, 4, 43–47,
    54–57, 59, 62, 69–70
Act 320 of 1911, 134
Adams, Lena, 63
Akhavan, Payam, 154
Alexander, Michelle, 68
Allwhite, Louis, 67
Allwhite, Newton, 67
Anderson, Kjell, 75, 77
anonymous victims, 28–29, 83
anti-miscegenation laws, 128–29,
    130–33, 134
Appeal, The, 121–22
Apperson, S. M., 99–100
Arkansas Democrat, 40, 53,
    84–85, 117–20 123–24
Arkansas Gazette, 44–45, 47, 76,
    117, 132–33; letters, 48–49,
    112, 113–16
Arkansas Gazette lynching
    reports: Bailey, George,
    30; Blakely, Joe, 54; Bays,
    Glenco, 109; Clarendon,
    Ark., 113; Coy, Edward, 141–
    46; Davis, Lovett, 53; Dodd,
    Frank, 40; Formosa, 46;
    Hicks, Robert, 126; Hogan,
    John, 111–12; Hot Springs,
    Ark., 63, 67; James, Henry,

97–98, 99, 101; Jeffries,
    Oscar, 124–25; Livingston,
    Frank, 109; Lowery, Henry,
    73–74; Marche, Ark., 29;
    Newport, Ark., 67; Pine
    Bluff, Ark., 53; St. Charles,
    Ark., 14–15, 41–42; Warren,
    Will, 31; Woodman, Joe, 124
Arkansas General Assembly,
    47, 66
Arkansas House of
    Representatives, 46, 48
Arkansas National Guard, 38,
    46, 55, 62, 63
Arkansas Senate, 44, 46, 48
Arkansas Supreme Court,47,
    63–64, 129, 134
assassination, 8, 159
Association of Southern
    Women for the Prevention
    of Lynching (ASWPL),
    17–18, 158
Atkins, Jerry, 107

Bailey, Abe, 41
Bailey, George, 30–31
Bailey, J. M., 87
Bailey, Ollie, 87
Baldwin, Mack, 41
Baldwin, Will, 41
Bays, Glenco, 108–9
Bellamy, Alex J., 21
Bennett, Idelle, 61
Bennett, Dave, 61
Bethel African Methodist
    (AME) Church (Little
    Rock, Ark.), 38

mimetic theory, 74, 136–41
Mississippi County, Ark., 71,
   73–74
Monroe County, Ark., 112–13
Morality of Groups, The, 22
Mosaic Templars of America, 38
mulattoes, 131–32, 139
Myrdal, Gunnar, 19

National Association for the
   Advancement of Colored
   People (NAACP), 17–18
National Memorial for Peace
   and Justice, 1
Negro Boys Industrial school,
   Wrightsville, Ark., 65–66, 68
Newport, Ark., 67
newspapers, 111
9th Street, Little Rock, Ark.,
   38, 39–40
Norman, Will, 54
Nuremberg trials, 78

objective violence, 57–67, 160
Oklahoma, 2
Oldham, Kie, 47–48
Ore, Ersula J., 50, 158
Orr, John, 112–13
Orr, Mabel, 112–13
overstating harm, practice of, 154

Padgett, Knowlton, 52
Palaver, Wolfgang, 27, 74, 136–
   38, 141, 145
Palmer, Paul C., 133
Paragould, Ark., 94
Patterson, Orlando, 148
Pennington (Mrs.), 98–99
Perner, Josef, 91
Pfeifer, Michael J., 51
Phillips County, Ark., 2, 107
Philpot, C. M., 52–53
Pickens, William, 60

Pickett, Henry, 45–46
Pickett, Wilson, 45–46
Pierce, Michael, 93
Pine Bluff, Ark., 52–53, 67, 95
Pine Bluff Daily Graphic, 84
Poe, Harry, 63–64
Poinsett County, Ark., 94
political violence, 62, 64, 69–70
Polk County, Ark., 94
poll tax, 59
Portland, Ark., 54
practical alienation, 23
Prairie County, Ark., 30–31
property crimes, 148
Pudd'nhead Wilson, 25
Pulaski County, Ark., 65–66
Pythian Hall, Little Rock,
   Ark., 101

race defined, 24–25, 27
race riot, 19–20, 38, 42
racial groups, 24–25, 27
Rai, Tage Shakti, 4–5, 101–6
rape trials, 133
Rast, Joe, 134–35
Rast, John, 134–35
Republic, 145–46
Republican Party, 130–33
Ricord, Dennis, 112–13
Rives, Ark., 123–24
Robb, Howard, 48
Robinson, Charles F., 128–29
Rothberg, Michael, 64–65
Ruck, Charles Spurgeon,
   55–56, 64
Rushdy, Ashraf H. A., 17–18,
   134, 149–50, 152–53,
   159–60
Ryan, John, 18, 21, 27
Ryan, Lyndall, 20

Salam, Ziya Us, 28
Sanders, Will, 113